Through Their Eyes

**40 DAYS OF CELEBRATING THE BIRTH OF
JESUS THROUGH THE EYES OF
THE FIRST CHRISTMAS PEOPLE**

Kellye Jones

Published by Hear My Heart Publishing

Copyright© 2016 by Kellye Jones

I dedicate this book to my Lord and Savior Jesus Christ. Thank you for entering the darkness of this world to bring the light of salvation to all people.

To God our Creator. Thank you for sending Your one and only Son into this world to save us and give us eternal life.

To my husband, Kevin Jones. You are my biggest cheerleader. You are the one who encourages me to pursue my dream of writing.

To my children who are my honest editors.

This book is written in memory of my dad, James Guy. He was my storyteller. I know he is in heaven listening to the author and perfector of our faith weave an incredible story of ultimate triumph.

Thanks to Beth Wilson of Hear My Heart Publishing. Thank you for taking a chance on this unknown writer.

Advent Season
Awaiting the Arrival

"But when the set time had fully come, God sent his Son,
born of a woman, born under the law, to redeem those under the
law, that we might receive adoption to son ship"
Galatians 4:4-5 NIV.

Waiting the Arrival

First Sunday of Advent
Day One

"And again, Isaiah says, 'The Root of Jesse will spring up, one who will arise to rule over the nations; in him the Gentiles will hope'" Romans 15:12 NIV.

"In that day the Root of Jesse will stand as a banner for the peoples; the nations will rally to him, and his resting place will be glorious" Isaiah 11:10 NIV.

"A shoot will come up from the stump of Jesse; from his roots a Branch will bear fruit" Isaiah 11:1 NIV.

"So the Lord God said to the serpent, "Because you have done this, "Cursed are you above all livestock and all wild animals! You will crawl on your belly and you will eat dust all the days of your life. And I will put enmity between you and the woman, and between your offspring and hers; he will crush your head, and you will strike his heel" Genesis 3:14-15 NIV.

I love this season. Many in Christendom call it the Advent Season. It begins the fourth Sunday before Christmas. Advent is the period of preparation for the celebration of the birth of Jesus. The word Advent comes from the Latin word "adventus," which means "coming." The definition of advent is the arrival of a notable person, thing, or event.

The nation of Israel has always had a deep heritage steeped in worship to Yahweh, The Great I AM. God had performed many miracles throughout their history. Their ancestors had seen seas and rivers part. Prophets of God had spoken and led the people, however there came a time of great silence from God. Caesar Augustus was ruler over their land. No longer was Israel under a theocratic government.

Israel felt abandoned by the One they worshipped. There hadn't been a prophet to speak the word of God since Malachi. In fact, the 400 years between the Old Testament and the New Testament are known as the "Silent Years." The last miracle Israel had witnessed was during the Maccabean Revolt. In 168 BC, the ruler of the Syrian kingdom, Antiochus Epephanes IV erected an idol on the altar of the temple in Jerusalem, and desecrated its holiness. A ragtag band of soldiers led by the Maccabean family drove out the Syrian legions using guerrilla warfare. During the war the Syrians stole the golden Menorah that burned continually in the temple before God. The Maccabee's made one of cheaper metal. When they wanted to light it, they found only a small cruse of pure olive oil. It was sufficient to light only for one day, but by a miracle of God, it continued to burn for eight days, till new oil was made available. This miracle proved God had again taken His people under His protection.

Then came the silence. For four hundred years no prophet spoke in Israel and no miracle from God had been performed for the sake of the nation. The nation of Israel was back in the Promise Land after years of exile, but they were under the domination of the great world power of the day, Rome. The temple had been restored after the exile, although it was a much smaller building than the one that Solomon had built and decorated in such marvelous glory. God seemed silent as the oppressive regime of Rome occupied Judea and kept her people under subjugation. The whole nation hoped and waited upon God's anointed One, their Messiah. He was the one Isaiah and many others prophesied about. This Messiah was the Hope of Israel and they were sure He would free them from Roman tyranny.

Notice I said, "God seemed silent." "Seemed" is the optimal word here. God is always at work around me as I learned from my study, 'Experiencing God' by Henry Blackaby. During these "silent years," God was preparing the earth for the coming of its Savior, His very own Son. God had allowed the Roman Empire to rise up and become the power kingdom of the known world. He used the dreaded Roman government to create a highway system that would drive the spread of the gospel from Jerusalem, to Judea, to Samaria, and eventually to the ends of the earth. The King of Heaven was preparing to wrap himself in the form of a newborn babe. The Son of God was about to leave the golden streets of heaven and travel the dusty roads of Roman territory.

Today marks the first Sunday of Advent. My husband and I like to light Advent Wreath Candles. The Advent Wreath is made up of five candles; three are purple, one is pink, and the middle one is white. The candles are lit each Sunday of December beginning the fourth Sunday before Christmas. The white candle represents the purity of Jesus. This is what we do to prepare our hearts for the true Reason for this Season, Our Savior, the Lord Jesus Christ. The first candle of this season is a purple candle. It is called "The Prophecy Candle" or "Candle of Hope."

I am currently walking through a trial that "seems" as if God is silent. I keep crying out to Him for deliverance. Today I light this candle because He is my hope. Jesus is still the Hope of Israel. I know God is always at work around me and because He sent His one and only Son into this world to save the people of this world, I have hope. I place my hope in the only One who will crush my true enemy underneath His foot. Many of my family and friends are hoping during this Advent Season. I am hoping with them. We are hoping for children battling adolescent cancer. We are hoping and praying for friends fighting terminal illnesses. Our hope is placed in Jesus Christ who goes before us to prepare for us a better place. We hope and pray...

And because my Hope is placed in the living God, I light this purple candle. God sent the Hope of Israel and fulfilled all the prophecies once before, why do I think all of a sudden He has become silent? God sent His one and only begotten Son two thousand years ago and all the nay-sayers were silenced. One dark and starry night, the King of Glory quietly entered our world and God filled the silence of hundreds of years with an angelic choir.

"Suddenly a great company of the heavenly host appeared with the angel, praising God and saying, Glory to God in the highest heaven, and on earth peace to those on whom his favor rests" Luke 2:13-14 NIV.

Questions to ponder and store in your heart:

What trial or struggle are you now facing that makes you cry out, "God, why are you being silent?"

What are some specific strategies you can strive for that will help you see God at work right now in the midst of this struggle?

What are your blessings right now even in the midst of your trials? Why not write them down, and then place them where they will be in your line of sight throughout this time?

How is God using this situation to draw you closer into His Presence?

Romans 8:25 in the NIV says, "But if we hope for what we do not yet have, we wait for it patiently." What is it you do not yet have? How is the waiting period going for you?

"But those who wait for the Lord's help find renewed strength; they rise up as if they had eagles' wings, they run without growing weary, they walk without getting tired." Isaiah 40:30 New English Translation. What are the promises of waiting?

"Lord, give me patience. Help me rise up on eagles' wings. My hope is in You. Amen."

Gabriel Comes Bearing News

Day Two

"While I, Daniel, was watching the vision and trying to understand it, there before me stood one who looked like a man. And I heard a man's voice from the Ulai calling, "Gabriel, tell this man the meaning of the vision." As he came near the place where I was standing, I was terrified and fell prostrate. "Son of man," he said to me, "understand that the vision concerns the time of the end." While he was speaking to me, I was in a deep sleep, with my face to the ground. Then he touched me and raised me to my feet" Daniel 8:15-18 NIV.

"While I was speaking and praying, confessing my sin and the sin of my people Israel and making my request to the Lord my God for his holy hill— while I was still in prayer, Gabriel, the man I had seen in the earlier vision, came to me in swift flight about the time of the evening sacrifice. He instructed me and said to me, Daniel, I have now come to give you insight and understanding. As soon as you began to pray, a word went out, which I have come to tell you, for you are highly esteemed. Therefore, consider the word and understand the vision" Daniel 9:20-23 NIV.

"Once when Zechariah's division was on duty and he was serving as priest before God, he was chosen by lot, according to the custom of the priesthood, to go into the temple of the Lord and burn incense. And when the time for the burning of incense came, all the assembled worshipers were praying outside.

Then an angel of the Lord appeared to him, standing at the right side of the altar of incense. When Zechariah saw him, he was startled and was gripped with fear. But the angel said to him: "Do not be afraid, Zechariah; your prayer has been heard. Your wife Elizabeth will bear you a son, and you are to call him John. He will be a joy and delight to you, and many will rejoice because of his birth, for he will be great in the sight of the Lord. He is never to take wine or other fermented drink, and he will be filled with the Holy Spirit even before he is born. He will bring back many of the people of Israel to the Lord their God. And he will go on before the Lord, in the spirit and power of Elijah, to turn the hearts of the parents to their children and the disobedient to the wisdom of the righteous—to make ready a people prepared for the Lord."

Zechariah asked the angel, "How can I be sure of this? I am an old man and my wife is well along in years." The angel said to him, "I am Gabriel. I stand in the presence of God, and I have been sent to speak to you and to tell you this good news. And now you will be silent and not able to speak until the day this happens, because you did not believe my words, which will come true at their appointed time" Luke 1:8-20 NIV.

The idea of this book was birthed during a time of great searching and contemplating the true meaning of Christmas. I love Christmas and all the days leading up to Christmas Day, but as I faced this particular Christmas season, I felt a melancholy sadness settle over me. I knew there were many reasons for these feelings and I wanted to get past them so I could sing, "Joy to the World" and mean it. No matter how hard I tried I couldn't pull myself up from the mire of my emotions. I plopped down in my favorite chair and cried out to God, "Please restore to me the joy of my salvation and the joy of this season!"

God led me back to those first Christmas people. Zachariah, Elizabeth, Gabriel, Mary, Joseph, Jesus, Simeon, and Anna became my long lost friends as I studied their stories. I began to write my thoughts on each one. I soon discovered their stories were also my story. Day by day I would read and write. Seven days into reading, studying, and writing about the events of that first Christmas, I realized, "I had my joy back!" I could sing, "Joy to the World" and mean it. Seven symbolizes a number of completeness. God had completely restored my Joy! I continued writing out each person's story. It took forty days. The number 40 represents a period of testing or trials.

It also means – a time of "proofing." Those forty days of writing had proofed my faith. I can now say with "Blessed Assurance" God works in our lives today. God hears our every prayer. God has a plan for each and every person. God is always at work around us.

So I get busy. I decorate for Christmas. It is what I routinely do every year during the week before Thanksgiving. Yes, I am one of those who put up Christmas before Thanksgiving. I am trying to shake myself out of this "Bah Humbug" type attitude. As I drag out each Christmas decoration, I remember to cherish the memories each decoration brings to my thoughts. My son and middle daughter have a hard time with this. They firmly believe no Christmas decorations until after Thanksgiving; my oldest daughter has inherited her mom's excitement and enchantment with Christmas. We like to have our decorations out as long as possible. I begin my playlist entitled "Christmas." I flood my home with Christmas worship by

Hillsong, Point of Grace, Avalon, and others. My playlist is long and distinguished.

I invite age old friends to come enjoy this advent season with me. I am enchanted with the people involved in the very first Christmas. I have been studying their stories for many years now. I love to hear their story as they recite for me what it was like that first Christmas so long ago. Let's close our eyes and listen as they retell their testimony of what they witnessed one starry night when the King of Glory entered our world.

I begin with Gabriel, the messenger angel. Do you ever wonder? Do you ever ask? Do angels question the path of God? If they do, I would think Gabriel must have. Below is my version of what I think happened as God prepared to unveil His Story.

The Messenger is Summoned

Gabriel, God's messenger Angel, was summoned to appear before the Most High. He quickly dropped all he was doing so that he could make an appearance before the Majesty of Heaven and Earth. He had delivered the Lord God's message to earth upon many occasions. He was a trusted delivery agent for the Most High. Now, he was summoned once again. All of heaven had awaited this glorious message. The electricity of the news was apparent in the heavenly realm. A grand plan of salvation was the buzz among each of the cherubim and seraphim. They had seen the twinkle in His Majesty's eyes. The Son of God was preparing and readying himself for departure. The angels weren't quite sure of the details, but they knew the fate of all mankind rested upon The Majesty's Son. Gabriel was given his first message and he instantly flew to do the Creator's bidding.

I am glad God didn't create me to be one of his angels because most definitely I would have asked, "Are you sure I should go to that ordinary priest down there? Isn't there a more miraculous and spectacular plan than this? Why are you going to use this old priest and his old wife to become involved with the entrance of Your Son into this dark world?"

Gabriel, this messenger angel, had been called upon once or twice before. In those instances, he had delivered God's message to a great prophet of God, Daniel. Daniel was a devout Jewish leader among the exiles in Babylon. Daniel had been disturbed about some dreams he had been having. He had been agonizing many days over these visions. He had fallen to his knees in prayer and fasting to discover their meaning. Gabriel had been sent to Daniel to deliver God's message concerning everything that He had revealed to Daniel.

Once again Gabriel was called upon to deliver a message. Gabriel flew swiftly do the Master's bidding. He stood before this aged priest who was performing the act of burning incense in the Most Holy Place. He delivered the message of the Lord. He towered above Zechariah at the right side of the Alter of Incense and Zachariah's eyes were opened to Gabriel's presence. Zachariah's initial response was fear. In fact, he was gripped with fear. This tells me Gabriel's presence was awe-inspiring. Gabriel was not the picture of a cute little cherub shooting love darts on Valentine's Day. His presence invoked fear in the ones to whom he was sent.

I have a few figurines of angels amongst my Christmas decorations. As I put them out, I am reminded of Zachariah's reaction on his encounter with the messenger angel Gabriel.

What would my reaction be if God determined that my eyes should be opened to see His angelic beings that are part of the Spiritual Realm surrounding me? I think my reaction would be the same as Zachariah's. I would also be gripped with fear.

I know my reality is, "there are unseen forces at battle all around me." My God is for me. I know those who are with me are greater than those who oppose me. God is the Lord of the angel armies. He has a message He needs me to understand. It is all written down for me in His word.

"When the servant of the man of God got up and went out early the next morning, an army with horses and chariots had surrounded the city. "Oh no, my Lord! What shall we do?" the servant asked. "Don't be afraid," the prophet answered. "Those who are with us are more than those who are with them." And Elisha prayed, "Open his eyes, Lord, so that he may see." Then the Lord opened the servant's eyes, and he looked and saw the hills full of horses and chariots of fire all around Elisha" 2 Kings 6:15-17 NIV.

I read these stories in the Word of God. I tell myself, "This is the reality that I cannot see." There is an unseen battle going on all around us every moment of the day. God is the Commander in Chief of the Angel Armies. There is a nest of vipers creatures at war against God's army. According to the verses in 2 Kings, I need not fear because those who are for us are greater than those who are against us. "He who is in me is greater than he who is in the world" 1 John 4:4.

Do you have angels among your Christmas decorations? If you do, as you set them in the place of your choosing, reflect on what it must have been like for Zachariah to see the angel Gabriel on the very first Christmas. What would you do if your Christmas decoration angels sprang up before you filling up the atmosphere of your home to announce a very important message from the Most High God?

Questions to ponder and store in your heart:

Gabriel's appearance to Zechariah in Luke 1 was not his first appearance to a human.

Read Daniel 8:15-19. Who stood in front of Daniel as he was praying?

Read Daniel 9:20-23 and Daniel chapter 10. Why was Gabriel sent once again to Daniel?

Read 2 Kings 6:15-17. What did Elisha's servant see after God opened his eyes?

What are your thoughts about the unseen battle between the army of God and Satan's demons that is raging all around us?

Do you believe angels are around you?

After reading all these verses we can be sure God is fighting for us, and He has an angelic army engaged in an unseen battle against an enemy set on destroying God's creation.

"Lord, open my eyes so that I might see the hills full of Your Warrior Angels."

He Hears Our Prayers

Day Three

"Because he bends down to listen, I will pray as long as I have breath." Psalm 116:2

"In the time of Herod, king of Judea, there was a priest named Zechariah, who belonged to the priestly division of Abijah; his wife Elizabeth was also a descendant of Aaron. Both of them were righteous in the sight of God, observing all the Lord's commands and decrees blamelessly. But they were childless because Elizabeth was not able to conceive, and they were both very old" Luke 1:5-7 NIV.

Meet my friend Zechariah. I am so thankful God's Word and His Story is filled with people like me. People whose faith isn't what I would call stellar, firm, and rock solid. God's Word is filled with heroes that need a little "something, something" to help them along in their faith. They need a little proof. Gideon to Doubting Thomas, and now Zechariah. I love him. I identify with him. I consider him my spiritual grandpa.

Let's look at how God described him. First, he and his wife were righteous in the sight of God. They observed all the Lord's commands and decrees blamelessly. He was a priest in the temple of the Lord. He was a descendant of Abijah. He was right up there in the spiritual pecking order. The Message Bible says they enjoyed a clear conscience before God.

The first phrase that describes Zechariah is "belonged to the priestly division of Abijah." Abijah was appointed priest by the great King David. Abijah was a descendant of Eleazar, the son of the very first high priest Aaron, brother of Moses. The priests were set apart for special ministries in the Temple in regards to the worship of God. Zachariah's name means, "Yahweh remembers." To say that Zechariah had credentials is putting it mildly. He and Elizabeth were pillars in the service of the Lord. They should have been esteemed among their peers. But... "But they were childless because Elizabeth was not able to conceive, and they were both very old."

Even with all their goodness and righteousness and clear conscience and spiritual credentials, these two had unanswered prayer. In their world and society children were seen as God's reward for faithful service. In those days you would have been looked down on if you were childless, especially if you were of old age and childless. Elizabeth would have been shunned at the prayer gatherings for the women of the church. Zechariah would have been talked about in each priestly circle. The gossip groups would have gone wild whispering about what sin Elizabeth and Zechariah must have committed that they are now without child. Surely they must have done some great unspeakable thing against the Lord because He is most definitely not answering their prayer. Did Zechariah and Elizabeth wonder, "Are we not faithful enough?" Did they question if they had dishonored God in some way? Even through their righteousness and all their goodness and faithfulness, heartache had invaded their home. Elizabeth ached to hold a child in her arms.

As these thoughts swirl in my head, I feel the Lord is speaking right to me. Just the other night I wondered if my prayers were floating higher than the ceiling. I have asked the question, "Lord do I have any unconfessed sin. Am I not faithful enough? Have I dishonored you in some way?"

Some days I do let my enemy into my thoughts. I hear the half-truths, "You did mess up. Let me remind you of all the ways." I let my enemy make me forget the healing power of God's grace. I hear the lie, "This is why you have unanswered prayer," and I forget the promise, "If we confess our sins God is faithful and just to forgive us our sins and purify us from all unrighteousness." I seem to think God answers my prayer based on my works. I forget He hears every cry of the brokenhearted. I do this every time it feels like God is not answering my prayer. "Really God? Really? What must I do to get you to listen to me?" God's answer, "Nothing, nothing at all. Do you trust me? Really, do you trust I love you with a love so great I sacrificed my only Son for you?" That is the question My God asks of me after I ask all my selfish questions.

This is the first lesson I learn from my good friend Zechariah. If this righteous, devout man and his wife with all their spiritual credentials had seemingly unanswered prayer, well, that brings me great hope. "Seem" is the optimum word here. I think it will be my buzzword for this whole month. "Seemingly, Seem." Seem means "give the impression or sensation of being or having a particular quality." What seems to me to be apparent truth, God says, "What appears to be truth in your realm is not what is truth in My Realm, and My Truth is the Ultimate Truth." What Zechariah perceived as unanswered prayer was truly God's "Wait answer." It was His "perfect timing" answer. It was His "exceedingly, abundantly above all we can ask, think, or imagine" answer.

Questions to ponder and store in your heart:

What in your life seems like an unanswered prayer?

What questions are you asking as you face what seems to be unanswered prayer?

What thoughts do you allow that causes the enemy to bring condemnation down onto you?

Read all of Zechariah's story in Luke 1. What is the promise you need to cling to from his story? Write it down. Store it in your heart. Declare it out loud and now own it.

Write out your prayer to the Lord

"Lord, thank you that there is now no condemnation for those who are in Christ Jesus. Thank you that you hear our every prayer."

God's Sense of Smell

Day Four

"In the time of Herod king of Judea there was a priest named Zechariah, who belonged to the priestly division of Abijah; his wife Elizabeth was also a descendant of Aaron. Both of them were righteous in the sight of God, observing all the Lord's commands and decrees blamelessly. But they were childless because Elizabeth was not able to conceive, and they were both very old. Once when Zechariah's division was on duty and he was serving as priest before God, he was chosen by lot, according to the custom of the priesthood, to go into the temple of the Lord and burn incense. And when the time for the burning of incense came, all the assembled worshipers were praying outside" Luke 1:5-10 NIV.

I can not leave this Holy Place. I know God wants to reveal to me many more truths as I observe this scene in Luke 1. I can vividly picture Zechariah lighting the Altar of Incense in my mind's eye. I have my shoes off because "Surely the Presence of the Lord is in this place" and I am on Holy Ground.

Let me set this stage according to the command of the Lord:

"Place the incense altar just outside the inner curtain that shields the Ark of the Covenant, in front of the Ark's cover—the place of atonement—that covers the tablets inscribed with the terms of the covenant. I will meet with you there. Every morning when Aaron maintains the lamps, he must

17

burn fragrant incense on the altar. And each evening when he lights the lamps, he must again burn incense in the Lord's presence. This must be done from generation to generation" Exodus 30:6-8 NLT.

"Then the Lord said to Moses, "Take fragrant spices—gum resin, onycha, and galbanum—and pure frankincense, all in equal amounts, and make a fragrant blend of incense, the work of a perfumer. It is to be salted and pure and sacred. Grind some of it to powder and place it in front of the Ark of the Covenant law in the tent of meeting, where I will meet with you. It shall be most holy to you. Do not make any incense with this formula for yourselves; consider it holy to the Lord. Whoever makes incense like it to enjoy its fragrance must be cut off from their people" Exodus 30:34-38 NIV.

I want to share with you a character trait of God that blows my mind.

GOD HAS A SENSE OF SMELL.

"Then Noah built an altar to the Lord, and there he sacrificed as burnt offerings the animals and birds that had been approved for that purpose. And the Lord was pleased with the aroma of the sacrifice and said to Himself, "I will never again curse the ground because of the human race, even though everything they think or imagine is bent toward evil from childhood. I will never again destroy all living things" Genesis 8:20-21.

Did you see it? Did you see the phrase "the Lord was pleased with the aroma of the sacrifice?" I have never really thought about that. God can smell aromas. I do not know why I haven't ever realized that. We are created in His image. We can smell the aromas of a freshly baked apple pie. I love the smell of honeysuckle blooming, so of course our Creator would be able to smell the aroma of meat cooking, because we can smell a roast baking in the oven for Sunday dinner.

The scene we read about in Luke 1 was of Zechariah being chosen by lot to go into the Holy Place and light the Alter of Incense. This was an established ordinance given by God to Moses. God commanded the priests to burn incense on the golden altar every morning and evening at the same time that the daily burnt offerings were made. The incense was to be left burning continually throughout the day and night as a pleasing aroma to the Lord. The incense was a symbol of the prayers and intercession of the people going up to God as a sweet fragrance.

Zechariah would have washed thoroughly, signifying his purification. This act of lighting the incense was the most honorable in this whole ceremony. He alone would have entered behind the curtain. After lighting the incense, Zachariah went to the task of intercession for his people. Zachariah prostrated himself in prayer before that altar. God wanted His dwelling to be a place where people could approach Him and pray to Him. The picture of prayer wafting up to heaven like incense is captured in David's psalm and also in John's vision in Revelation:

"May my prayer be set before you like incense; may the lifting up of my hands be like the evening sacrifice" Psalm 141:2.

"Another angel, who had a golden censer, came and stood at the alter. He was given much incense to offer, with the prayers of all the saints, on the golden altar before the throne. The smoke of the incense, together with the prayers of the saints, went up before God from the angel's hand" Revelation 8:3.

God is an amazing Author. His description of His Alter of Incense paints such a vivid picture I can actually be with Zechariah as he is lighting the incense. The pious and faithful Jews were gathered in the temple courts because it was time for the evening sacrifice and the lighting of the lamps. They had come knowing the priest would burn the incense as a representation of their prayers rising to heaven. Zechariah's wife Elizabeth would have also been watching with pride as her man wore his blue robe and stepped behind the curtain to the Holy Place. She, too, would have been offering up her silent pleas for a child yet given to her.

I tell this story as I see it unfolding in my mind's eye from the vantage point of the Most High God:

The Lord is Gracious

"El Elyon, The Most High, The Only God, sat perched on His throne. He had prepared all things. The time was drawing nigh. He could already feel the absence of His One and Only Son who was sitting at His right side. They had prepared together and now all the forces were gathering like a mighty rushing wind. God had caused the lot to fall to this aged priest. Zechariah had been chosen to play an integral part in God's plan to save the world before the foundations of the world had been laid. God had heard the prayers of this righteous man and his wife for many years.

The babe had been in God's creative hand since the plan of salvation had been hatched between Him and His Son. God had even given the child a name, "John." It means, "The Lord is Gracious." The stage was set. It was time. The one who would prepare the way for His Son was about to be announced to his soon to be parents. God called Zechariah to the quiet place, to an alone place, a place where it would only be Him and the soon to be father. The aroma drifted upward. The most high God smelled the pleasing fragrance. He saw, He heard, and He felt each prayer of His people gathered to pray. He heard her heartache. He had felt it year after year. Now He would tell Elizabeth, "The Most High had not forgotten her." He heard her pleas for many years now, but He just had a perfect timing and an "exceedingly abundantly great answer." He was about to do something in her life that only He could do. "Gabriel," God summoned as the pleasing aroma of incense and prayers filled the throne room. "I have a mission for you..."

God has a sense of smell. It is hard to wrap my mind around that concept. I really don't know why. We are created in His image. I guess it is another aspect of God that endears me to Him. He created my grandson, Lucas, with a great sense of smell. Lucas loves the fragrances of Christmas. (Actually, he loves a lot of pleasing aromas just like my Heavenly Father.) I gave him "Cool Breeze" hand sanitizer yesterday. He wanted to try my "Green Apple." He came over and wanted to smell my electric Christmas incense that burns continually during Advent Season. Really, these aromas bring great pleasure to Lucas. Lucas' reaction is a reminder to me that my prayers and sacrifices are a pleasing aroma to the Lord God. So why am I not offering them up to Him continually as the decree of the Alter of Incense suggests?

Questions to ponder and store in your heart:

What does the Psalmist say about his prayer in Psalm 141:2?

What does John say about prayer in Revelation 8:3-4?

In Genesis 8:20-21, what did God do when He smelled the pleasing sacrifice of Noah?

Close your eyes and take time today to offer up to God your sacrifice of prayer; then mentally see your prayer rising as incense before Him. That is what God's Word says of our prayers. Do the foul smells of selfishness, bitterness, anger, or unforgiveness hinder your incense?

"Lord, purify me of any unrighteousness. Create in me a pure heart O God and give me a renewed spirit to obey you. May my life become a pleasing aroma to You."

The Sound of Silence

Day Five

"One day Zechariah was serving God in the Temple, for his order was on duty that week. As was the custom of the priests, he was chosen by lot to enter the sanctuary of the Lord and burn incense. While the incense was being burned, a great crowd stood outside, praying. While Zechariah was in the sanctuary, an angel of the Lord appeared to him, standing to the right of the incense altar. Zechariah was shaken and overwhelmed with fear when he saw him.

But the angel said, "Don't be afraid, Zechariah! God has heard your prayer. Your wife, Elizabeth, will give you a son, and you are to name him John. You will have great joy and gladness, and many will rejoice at his birth, for he will be great in the eyes of the Lord. He must never touch wine or other alcoholic drinks. He will be filled with the Holy Spirit, even before his birth. And he will turn many Israelites to the Lord their God. He will be a man with the spirit and power of Elijah. He will prepare the people for the coming of the Lord. He will turn the hearts of the fathers to their children, and he will cause those who are rebellious to accept the wisdom of the godly."

Zechariah said to the angel, "How can I be sure this will happen? I'm an old man now, and my wife is also well along in years." Then the angel said, "I am Gabriel! I stand in the very presence of God. It was he who sent me to bring you this good news! But now, since you didn't believe what I said, you will be silent and unable to speak until the child is born. For my words will certainly be fulfilled at the proper time" Luke 1:8-20 NLT.

"Six days later, Jesus took Peter and the two brothers, James and John, and led them up a high mountain to be alone. As the men watched, Jesus' appearance was transformed so that his face shone like the sun, and his clothes became as white as light. Suddenly, Moses and Elijah appeared and began talking with Jesus. Peter exclaimed, "Lord, it's wonderful for us to be here! If you want, I'll make three shelters as memorials —one for you, one for Moses, and one for Elijah." But even as he spoke, a bright cloud overshadowed them, and a voice from the cloud said, "This is my dearly loved Son, who brings me great joy. Listen to him" Matthew 17:1-5 NL.

Do you do that with God? Talk, talk, talk, and don't listen, listen, listen? If you do, join the club, and guess what? We are not alone. Great pillars of our faith have forged that path before us. As we see in these verses, Peter and Zechariah are guilty also.

Two people whom I love to listen to ramble on, are my grandsons, Asher and Lucas. Some days I get to pick them up from school. From the momen t they get into the car both boys speak at the same time. Their incessant chatter became my fondest memory. I have had drives when I seriously don't think they stopped to take a breath. Literally, it is a continual sentence from school to home. When they are both buckled in the backseat it is like they are jockeying for conversation time.

My daughter has been given the gift of listening to two completely different conversations at the same time and actually following the chain of events. I am trying to hone that skill. It takes great concentration. Their chatter is a pleasant sound to my ears. They are both very gifted storytellers. I wouldn't even dream of trying to carry on a conversation of my own with my daughter at the same time. Their prattle is too precious to me. I don't want to miss a single word.

I wonder if that is how God feels about me? I definitely have the gift of talking incessantly at God. I know He loves to engage in dialogue with me, but He wants it to be a two-way street. I contemplate the sentence I just wrote. Two words seem highlighted - **"at God."** Sometimes my prayers are a one sided conversation. I am talking "At God" not "to Him." It is like I am trying to counsel Him on how to best handle my situation. I tend to think I am the wisest one in this relationship. My prayer life is like the gift of gab. I need to tell the Creator of the Universe how to do His job. Hmmmm? I realize I am like Zechariah and Peter. There is a T-shirt out that was made especially for each of us. The front says, "Help, I'm talking and I can't shut up." God once spoke to Peter, "This is my dearly loved Son who brings me great joy. *Listen to Him!"*

As Zechariah stepped behind the first curtain and walked into the Holy Place, he would have kept walking right up to the curtain that separated the Holy Place from the Holy of Holy Place, for the Alter of Incense was placed right in front of this curtain. He would have begun trimming all the lamps. He would have fanned into flame once again the incense of the altar so that its smoke would have continually risen before God.

It was here, while he was doing his God appointed mission that the divine appointment happened for Zechariah. At this moment, Heaven touched earth on the right side of the

Alter of Incense. Gabriel appeared to Zechariah. Gabriel's name means "Strength of God." God opened Zechariah 's eyes to see beyond the thin veil that separates the physical realm from the spiritual realm. That doesn't happen often to us human folk. I think it is because God knows it would scare the "heebeegeebees" out of us. When Zechariah saw him, he was startled and overcome with fear.

Again, Gabriel isn't our picture of a sweet little cherub. The Message Bible describes Gabriel as "The Sentinel of God." The Voice Bible says, "The Messenger who inhabits God's Presence." God was with Zechariah in this Holy Place while Zechariah was serving Him.

When Moses encountered the Presence of God, he had to cover his face because the Glory of God radiated from it. When this Angel appeared to Zechariah, I believe God's Glory had to be as overwhelming as it had been for Moses. You can bet that it bowled the poor man over. I wonder if he worried about a heart attack. He tried to explain to Gabriel the obvious. "I am an old man. How can I know this? Oh and by the way, in case God the Creator didn't realize this, my wife is beyond child bearing age also." Yep, stating the obvious.

Have you ever done that with God? State all the obvious reasons why this certain situation is occurring, and why all God's promises can't possibly apply here? Do you have a tendency to talk non-stop when you are scared? Boy, I do. That is what Zechariah was doing at this moment. Talk. Talk. Talk. He was scared.

But Gabriel had had enough prattle from this old priest. Again God's Word rings out, **NOW LISTEN!** These were strong words, strongly spoken. And when Gabriel spoke the next words "You will become silent." those words were spoken with such power they did take away Zechariah's speech.

Literally Zechariah would exit the Holy Place living in "The Sound of Silence."

I think that would be a terrible hardship on me not to be able to talk or hear. I couldn't listen to my grandson's conversations. That would not be good. But what appears to me to be a terrible hardship is a blessing in disguise. God's discipline is always like that. It appears horrible from our vantage point, but from God's perspective it produces in us righteousness we cannot attain apart from His discipline.

I wonder did Zechariah try to speak back to the Mighty Angel? Can you imagine his feelings of horror as he opened his mouth and no sound came forth? God would have no more talking from this aged priest until the promise was birthed. God definitely wasn't going to let Zechariah's doubts infect Elizabeth who would become the carrier of the promise.

Do you know the greatest Christmas gift I carry away from this story of Zechariah's silence? My doubts will never negate God's promises. He will not allow my doubts and fears to steal the promises He has spoken into my life. I might have to live in silence for a while, but God's Word will be enacted in my life. God's Word will never return to Him void.

Questions to ponder and store in your heart:

What do you think is the difference between talking "at God" and "to God?'

God once told Peter, "This is my beloved Son. **LISTEN TO HIM!**" How can you actually stop talking at God and really stop and listen to Him?

How uncomfortable are you during the sound of silence while you are praying?

Do you know how to recognize God's voice? It is different for everyone.

What does it sound like to you?

"Lord, I come to You in the silence. Help me to listen to You."

Hold Onto the Promise

Day Six

"Then an angel of the Lord appeared to him, standing at the right side of the altar of incense. When Zechariah saw him, he was startled and was gripped with fear. But the angel said to him: "Do not be afraid, Zechariah; your prayer has been heard. Your wife Elizabeth will bear you a son, and you are to call him John. He will be a joy and delight to you, and many will rejoice because of his birth, for he will be great in the sight of the Lord. He is never to take wine or other fermented drink, and he will be filled with the Holy Spirit even before he is born. He will bring back many of the people of Israel to the Lord their God. And he will go on before the Lord, in the spirit and power of Elijah, to turn the hearts of the parents to their children and the disobedient to the wisdom of the righteous—to make ready a people prepared for the Lord" Luke 1:11-17 NIV.

"When it was time for Elizabeth to have her baby, she gave birth to a son. Her neighbors and relatives heard that the Lord had shown her great mercy, and they shared her joy. On the eighth day they came to circumcise the child, and they were going to name him after his father Zechariah, but his mother spoke up and said, "No! He is to be called John." They said to her, "There is no one among your relatives who has that name." Then they made signs to his father, to find out what he would like to name the child. He asked for a writing tablet, and to everyone's astonishment he wrote, "His name is John." Immediately his mouth was opened and his tongue set free, and he began to speak, praising God. All the neighbors were filled with awe, and throughout the hill country of Judea people were talking about all these things. Everyone who heard this wondered about it, asking, "What then is this child going to be?" For the Lord's hand was with him" Luke 1:57-66 NIV.

"When Elizabeth heard Mary's greeting, the baby leaped in her womb, and Elizabeth was filled with the Holy Spirit" Luke 1:41 NIV.

I said yesterday, "My doubts and fears cannot negate God's promises spoken into my life." Even after Zechariah spouted off all the obvious reasons why this spoken Word and Promise couldn't possibly come to be in Elizabeth's life and his, the Lord didn't say, "Oh okay. If you don't believe it then it won't happen." No! He took control of the situation. He took control of Zechariah's speech and hearing. These were all the parts in Zechariah that would cause doubt in God's Promise. When a terrible outcome came upon Zechariah, I.E. loss of speech and hearing, God turned it into a positive. God had the most important plan unfolding and He was not going to let an old priest's doubts steal part of the plan of salvation. The plan had already been set in motion. What I see as a negative situation, God used it to embolden Zechariah. Zechariah's deafness and muteness was the evidence he needed to hold onto the promises he had just heard.

PROMISES SPOKEN INTO ZECHARIAH'S LIFE
1. Your Prayer has been heard!
2. Your wife will bear you a son!
3. Name the child "John." John means, "Jehovah is

gracious" or "God has shown favor."
4. He will bring you great joy and gladness!
5. Many will rejoice at his birth!
6. He will be great in the Lord's sight!
7. He will be filled with the Holy Spirit even before he is born.
8. He will bring back many of the people of Israel to the Lord their God.
9. He will go on before the Lord, in the spirit and power of Elijah!
10. He will turn the hearts of the parents to their children and the disobedient to the wisdom of the righteous.
11. He will make ready a people prepared for the Lord!

It is like a checklist for Zechariah. I wonder if he did this; I wonder if he checked off each of these promises as they were fulfilled in his life? As I wrote out these spoken promises Gabriel evangelized into Zechariah's life that day beside the Alter of Incense, I thought, "WOW!"

Obviously, I read these promises from the backside of history, after they all came to be. I turn to Matthew chapter 3 and I see every single one of these words came to fulfillment in John's life! What on earth makes me question if God's Promises will ever be broken in my life?

The thing that inspires me in Zechariah's character after he entered the world of silence was Zechariah held onto the promises that he had heard from Gabriel when he still had his hearing. His disability only enhanced his grip on the promises. Even after he received them, Zechariah was still faithful to complete his service to God.

"When it's time of service was completed, he returned home. After this his wife Elizabeth became pregnant..." Luke 1:23-24a NIV.

Zechariah didn't take the fulfillment of the promise into his own hands and timing. He had been changed since the receiving of the promise, and he knew now to leave the timing to God. He stayed faithful to his service in the Temple of the Lord.

Somehow he was able to translate to his wife what had happened to him behind that curtain in the Holiest Place. Somehow Zachariah was able to describe to Elizabeth his great fear upon seeing Gabriel. Somehow he was able to convey to her the promise of their long awaited child. Zachariah was able to convince her this child was a boy and they should name him John, because that is what she stated before Zachariah had recovered his speech. Truly it was unheard of to name a child anything other than a family name. No one in either Elizabeth or Zechariah's family tree was named John. God had been gracious to her and Zechariah. He had shown them favor. Zechariah had been so changed by his encounter with God that day in the Temple; he was able to inspire his wife into believing in the promise despite his speech impediment!

That is what we do when we have God's Words implanted into our core, into our heart, into our belief system. We are given a power to inspire many to believe in the promises of God!

I challenge each of you this Advent Season:

Get alone with God!

Let Him speak a promise to you from His Word

Then hold onto that promise until it is fulfilled in your life!

Questions to ponder and store in your heart:

What does it mean to you to "hold onto the promise of God?"

Did you notice that after Zechariah received the promise he stayed and continued serving God? So often I want to run out immediately and help God's promise come into being. From Zechariah's example, what should we do when we receive a promise from God?

What are some practical steps we can take to hold onto the promises God stores in your heart?

So often doubt creeps into my mind and I think, "Now, did God really say this to me?" 2 Corinthians 10:5 says, "We demolish arguments and every pretension that sets itself up against the knowledge of God, and we take captive every thought to make it obedient to Christ." How can you keep doubt from stealing God's promise spoken into your life?

"Lord, keep me from taking matters into my own hands. I want Your promises to flow unheeded by my impatience. Guard me from doubting You."

Expecting the Holy

Day Seven

"Meanwhile, the people were waiting for Zechariah and wondering why he stayed so long in the temple. When he came out, he could not speak to them. They realized he had seen a vision in the temple, for he kept making signs to them but remained unable to speak" Luke 1:21-22 NIV.

This was a unique day for Zachariah. The priests serving in the Temple of God were divided into 24 groups or divisions of which Zechariah's division of Abijah would have been eighth in the rotation. This was the week Zechariah's division was serving. The priests and their families would live in Jerusalem or in various nearby villages, but when their division was called up for duty for a week, twice each year, the priests would come to Jerusalem to work in the Temple. Zechariah lived in the hill country of Judea. Each day about 50 priests would have been on duty, with perhaps 300 on duty during a given week. This day, Zechariah is chosen by lot to go inside the temple and burn incense on the altar.

Since there were such a large number of priests, no priest was allowed to serve as the officiating priest more than once in his lifetime. This is why I say this was a unique day. The odds of him being chosen by lot were astronomical, a one in a million chance. I am sure Zechariah would have felt the butterflies as he prepared for this auspicious and humbling task. He was prepared for a Holy Moment. He had been trained to treat this honorable job with reverence. However, as he entered the Holy Place I do not think he said, "I bet I see an angel today."

I really do not know what Zechariah was expecting as he stepped behind the veil. Zechariah recognized the uniqueness of being chosen. He knew it was a Divine Appointment. This was a task you did not take lightly. It was an honor to serve the Lord in this manner. His was a solemn task done with reverence to the most High God.

"As was the custom of the priests, he was chosen by lot to enter the sanctuary of the Lord and burn incense. While the incense was being burned, a great crowd stood outside, praying" Luke 1:9-10 NLT.

On the morning of the Holy Event, Zechariah would have donned his blue priestly tunic. Elizabeth would have made sure it was wrinkle free. He would have approached the curtain with reverence. A great crowd would have been there. He would have heard the murmurings of many prayers going up. He was expecting the Divine. He wasn't expecting the angel who stood in the very presence of the Most High God. Nevertheless, Zechariah did experience heaven touching earth when Gabriel appeared to him. He experienced a Holy Moment. The Presence of God in the Holy of Holies was palpable. Nothing in his training had prepared him for this moment.

He didn't handle the situation well. He didn't exhibit the poised priestly attitude he had been trained in. He saw Gabriel standing in might and power at the right side of the Altar of Incense. Fear took possession of him. No other priest had witnessed such a sight since the first High Priest, Aaron, the brother of Moses. Zechariah could hear the rush of Gabriel's entrance. The glory of the Lord was seen in his face.

He could physically feel God's power and grace. There was a holy hush behind the heavy veil. He could almost see God's face and touch the hem of His robe. Surely the Presence of the Lord was with him behind the veil. Words of God's promise were spoken to him and he exited the Holy Place changed and changed for the better. He entered with hearing and speech; he exited in silence. He exited with a disability, but the disability was a blessing. The people recognized he had been changed.

Today is Saturday. Tomorrow is Sunday. We Christians are preparing for the Lord's Day tomorrow. Do we go with expectations of having a Holy Moment? We should. Our time at church is a Divine Appointment set up by God. Surely the Presence of the Lord is in this place because He has promised where two or more are gathered in His name there He is with us. We should go to church prepared to have an encounter with the Great I Am. And when we exit, can people tell we have been changed? Can they see it in our countenance? They should. People will acknowledge our change when we are fully engaged in worship and the message we receive from our pastor. That is what hearing the Word of God spoken to us does. It changes us for the better. Zechariah came out a changed man. He had an encounter with the Lord at the temple in the Holy Place. He was totally engaged in his service to the Lord and the Lord met him there.

When we head to church this week, we should give a thought or two about Zechariah. Go expecting for the Presence of the Lord to show up. Engage in worship. Listen and take to heart to the word you hear. And then we will all be changed for the better because "Surely the Presence of the Lord" was in our service.

Questions to ponder and store in your heart:

Name one practical way you can engage in worship as you head to church.

How can you physically participate in worship at your church this week?

Do you expect a Holy Moment as you prepare for church this Sunday?

Do you remember certain services better than others? Why is that? Could it be on those days you did a better job of preparing your heart?

"Lord, prepare my heart for holy moments with You. Go before me this day and level all hills and mountains that might keep me from worshipping You."

The Candle of Preparation

The Second Sunday of Advent
Day Eight

"But you, O Bethlehem Ephrathah, are only a small village among all the people of Judah. Yet a ruler of Israel, whose origins are in the distant past, will come from you on my behalf" Micah 5:2 NLT.

"Jesus was born in Bethlehem in Judea, during the reign of King Herod" Matthew 2:1A NLT.

Today is the second Sunday in the Advent Season. Today I light the purple Bethlehem Candle. It is also known as the Candle of Preparation. I went to church this morning expecting to have a Holy Moment with God. I had many Holy Moments. God met me in exceedingly abundant ways I never dreamed possible. In worship I sang over and over again the words, "He split the seas so I could walk right through" and "I am a child of God." My pastor's message was, "How do I function in God's Silence?" Several points resonated in my heart, "God is more interested in the process than He is in the progress." "God is with me in the process." "The preparation makes me who I am." And then finally, "Great is Thy faithfulness, Great is Thy faithfulness."

I am an impatient person. Waiting is hard on me. When you are preparing for something you are also waiting for that event to happen. I am not fond of preparation. When I am hungry I want to eat immediately so preparing my food is a hardship for me. I would rather go through a drive thru, but that is not a wise choice for me. If I want to eat a nutritious meal I must take time to prepare fresh vegetables and lean protein. We are in a generation of immediate gratification. Seasons of preparation are hard, time consuming, and back breaking, but God's preparation time will make us into the creation He desires us to become.

So now I light the Candle of Preparation and it takes on whole new meaning for me. I am in a season of Preparation. This season is not fun. In fact it is hard and my heart breaks open daily. I am reminded this season of preparation has a purpose. My struggle is a gift from God. It is creating in me the character of holiness. God is with me, by my side, and ever present during this time. He is with me in this process. How I handle it will shape me into the person I will become. The question I must constantly ask myself, "How am I handling this preparation time? Am I complaining as the Israelites did as they traveled through the wilderness or am I allowing God to perfect holiness and endurance in me?"

Every single one of us has experienced, or we are experiencing, or will experience again, a season of Preparation from God. It is not *if* you will experience it but *when* you will experience it. God prepared Jesus for thirty years before Jesus set out for ministry. God prepared Israel for centuries before He sent them their Messiah. God doesn't waste the preparation years. These times serve a purpose in each of our lives. These times have one desired response, that we should become more like Jesus. The tests of God do come, but God made them passable. They are open book tests. God lets us ask our neighbors for help. God even lets us ask "the teacher" for the answer. God is ever faithful.

"Yet this I call to mind and therefore I have hope: Because of the Lord's great love we are not consumed, for his compassions never fail. They are new every morning; great is your faithfulness. I say to myself, "The Lord is my portion; therefore, I will wait for him" Lamentations 3:21-24 NIV.

God remains faithful to us every single day in large circumstances and in small. God doesn't change. Every morning when we wake up, God's mercy and grace is new for us. God offers bright hope for us even while we are shrouded in dark times of worry. He pardons our sins and wrongdoings over and over again; then He points out the correct way to walk. His peace and completeness is ever before us. Truly, "Great is His Faithfulness!"

The church, the body of Christ, The Bride of Christ is also in a season of preparation. We are preparing for Jesus' return. He promised, "He will return. He is now preparing a home for us in heaven."

"Don't let your hearts be troubled. Trust in God, and trust also in me. There is more than enough room in my Father's home. If this were not so, would I have told you that I am going to prepare a place for you? When everything is ready, I will come and get you, so that you will always be with me where I am. And you know the way to where I am going" John 14:1-4 NLT.

"The master will return unannounced and unexpected" Matthew 24:50 NLT.

"In the same way, when you see all these things, you can know his return is very near, right at the door" Matthew 24:33 NLT.

Jesus was born in Bethlehem in Judea the first time He came to earth. He will return very soon. This time it will be anything but quiet. The sky will roll back and a trumpet will sound. His return will be unexpected, but it will happen. We must be prepared. The word, "prepare" means "to be ready!" We are in that season of preparation and as my pastor pointed out this morning, "During the season of preparation, we must be obedient."

Jesus warns over and over, "Be ready! Be obedient! Go out into all the world and make disciples!" We must be about the business of telling others about our Savior so that all will be ready for when the skies roll back and He comes riding in!

Questions to ponder and store in your heart:

If you are in a season of preparation, describe this season.

Write down the promises that God is answering in your life during this season.

What should we be doing while God is preparing us to be like Jesus?

What were the promises God made Abraham during this season in Genesis 17?

Did those promises come to fruition?

If you are in a season of preparation, what are the promises God is giving you?

What should we be doing while God is preparing us to be like Jesus?

"Lord, I want to rejoice overYou during the struggles of my life. Give me Your perspective, and make me more like Jesus."

The "Little Women of Christmas"

Day Nine

"How kind the Lord is!" Elizabeth exclaimed. "He has taken away my disgrace of having no children" Luke 1:25 NLT.

"Mary responded, "I am the Lord's servant. May everything you have said about me come true." And then the angel left her" Luke 1:38 NLT.

"Anna, a prophet, was also there in the Temple. She was the daughter of Phanuel from the tribe of Asher, and she was very old. Her husband died when they had been married only seven years. Then she lived as a widow to the age of eighty-four. She never left the Temple but stayed there day and night, worshiping God with fasting and prayer. She came along as Simeon was talking with Mary and Joseph, and she began praising God. She talked about the child to everyone who had been waiting expectantly for God to rescue Jerusalem" Luke 2:36-38 NLT.

Anna, Elizabeth, and Mary. God's own version of "Little Women." I call them "Little Women of Christmas." Three very different women from three very different generations formed a life of weaving a unique tapestry of a virtuous living. Each woman had her own style of wisdom and grace, and

43

each woman can teach me a lesson or two about being a godly lady, wife and mother.

It makes me think of my mom, myself, and my daughters and daughter-in-law. My mom's generation is known as the "Silent Generation." I had to look that up. The theory behind this label "Silent Generation" is the children who grew up during this time worked very hard and kept quiet. My generation is known as Gen X or the unknown generation. My daughters are Generation Y. They are the rise of the information age.

God has taught each of us different lessons through the years based on our own experiences and world events. One thing I have learned in my journey of walking with God, is each of us can learn a deep spiritual truth from other generations. We all come to know God as we experience Him in our different environments. No one person owns all the knowledge of God. We are part of a team. We are the body of Christ and we need each other. We need the golden nuggets of wisdom God deposits in all the varieties of His Kingdom. I need to hear the truths God has taught the "Silent Generation." I am a more rounded Christian and individual when I listen to the wisdom of "Generation Y," the Information Age.

Each of us has been filled with nuggets of wisdom taught to us by God through our various trials and environments and world events. We view certain passages of scripture through the eyes of our own experiences. We need to learn from the generations that surround our lives.

In the same manner we can learn a different spiritual truth from Anna, Elizabeth, and Mary. Bible scholars estimate the age of Anna to be over one hundred years old. Elizabeth was elderly, and Mary was a young teenager. These women came from differing backgrounds and world settings. Anna had been a widow for most of her adult life and chose to remain in that state. Elizabeth was unable to conceive during a time that her society viewed being sterile as a curse from God. Mary became pregnant at a time when the law says to stone a woman who conceived out of wedlock. This was a very divergent group of women, but each has a story to tell and a lesson to teach us.

Today I am only going to look at Elizabeth. I love her name. It means "Oath of God, or God's Oath." It means God is the Oath Keeper. I have an Elizabeth. My middle child is Magen Elizabeth. She was named after my husband's grandmother. Her first name means, "Shield." Literally Magen's name means "Shield of God's Oath." I love that. Her name speaks a thousand promises of God to me. Kevin, my husband, and I didn't know all this when we named her, but now looking back I see God's hand as we named each of our three children.

Now, knowing the meaning of "Elizabeth," I picture a regal woman. In my mind, as I think of Elizabeth, Laura Bush pops up. Elizabeth was regal but possessed a humble grace. She is my picture of a real Proverbs 31 lady. She was virtuous and capable. Zechariah trusted her. When he was in the limelight serving the Lord, she was in the shadows praying and serving her man. She greatly enriched his life. She was wise and energetic. She was righteous in God's eyes. She was careful to obey all of the Lord's commands, and somehow when Zechariah conveyed all he saw behind the veil to the Holy Place, she believed him with no hesitation. She nurtured the promise Zechariah had received.

"When Zechariah's week of service in the Temple was over, he returned home. Soon afterward his wife, Elizabeth, became pregnant and went into seclusion for five months. "How kind the Lord is!" she exclaimed. "He has taken away my disgrace of having no children" Luke 1:32-25.

Oh my goodness. Did you catch her grace and humility? When she received the fulfillment of that promise, she went into seclusion. She didn't go blabbing and stirring up conversation, and say, "Look I told you so." She went away with God and let Him nurture the promise. I am absolutely blown away with the royal beauty those words paint for me. She is my own personal "Queen Elizabeth of quiet grace and humbleness." She didn't want to do anything after receiving the Promise but get in seclusion and worship the Only One who could fulfill that promise.

"How kind the Lord is!" she said with an exclamation mark. The Lord was enough for her at that moment. She didn't need the affirmations or acclamations of other women. God had blessed her with an amazing gift. He had given her something only He could give, so she grasped hold of the Gift Giver with both hands and honored Him by sitting at His feet and offering Him worship and thanksgiving. She wanted to breathe in this fulfillment of a promise. Truly I have no words. Sometimes words seem to muddy up the beauty of the moment. I should follow her example. I should just sit and worship, shut out the world around me, go into seclusion and worship the One who died for me and gave me new life.

Questions to ponder and store in your heart:

What are some spiritual truths you have learned from other generations?

Describe Elizabeth.

What did Elizabeth do when she became pregnant?

What do we need to do when God fulfills a promise to us?

"Lord, I humble myself before You. Thank you for surrounding me with such a great cloud of witnesses. Help me to learn from those who have gone before me and those who are coming behind me."

God Has Taken Away My Disgrace

Day Ten

"When Zechariah's week of service in the Temple was over, he returned home. Soon afterward his wife, Elizabeth, became pregnant and went into seclusion for five months. "How kind the Lord is!" she exclaimed. He has taken away my disgrace of having no children" Luke 1:23-25.

Okay. I am going to lay it out there for you. I am going to get real with you. I would rather eat dirt than put myself out there and expose all my vulnerabilities and write this book. By nature I am a private person. It is hard to expose all my struggles and insecurities when I write some of these chapters. These Christmas people and their stories have become my story. I see my fears and failures written out through their eyes.

I would rather keep the lessons the Lord has taught me to myself. I really don't want to put my insecurities out there, and believe me, that is what I told the Lord when He asked me to write. I remember it clearly. I was at a writing conference, and I walked through the halls debating with God in each class I took. I walked with my arms crossed and my mentality stubborn. "I am not going to put myself out there, God. I am not and You can't make me."

I won't bore you with the back and forth dialogue I had with God, but needless to say I laid out every valid argument I could think of. I stated my case like a professional lawyer. Do you want to know the verdict of my arguments? Nine months later I am sitting here writing my first book. I lost my court case with "The Judge" of all the earth. My lead argument with Him was, " Lord, I am not all that stable. At times my faith is very shaky. Who am I to encourage people in the faith? Really, You have handled many meltdowns from me. You know first hand all the doubts I have shouted toward the heavens. I can't encourage people in the faith, especially my family and friends. They have witnessed too many of my mess ups!" Or, " Lord I can't serve in Ethiopia. I am getting too old for this. You do know I am over 50 now."

Is it me, or do I sound like Zechariah to you also? I love stating the obvious to the Lord. Zechariah and I have this need to fill God in on the status of our lives. He is the God of the universe. He does not sleep nor does He slumber. He knows my every thought. This was His judgment as I finished my closing arguments, "No one is too old to serve. I am the One who gave you your love of writing. I am the One who fills your thoughts with my words. Your writing is your form of worship to Me. You just write. I will be the One to increase your faith." So I write and He is faithful. Every time I sit down at this keyboard He sends me a promise or a word that I feel is designed for me and for the situation that I am facing. Every time I write an article it is like I am sitting down for a counseling session with the Ultimate Counselor and it's free!

So Elizabeth's words become my words. "How kind the Lord is! He has taken away my disgrace." I may not be a pillar of faith but I am a work in progress and according to Philippians 1:6, "He who began a good work in me will be faithful to complete it." God has filled my disgrace with His Grace.

You may have tried that argument a time or two with "The Judge."

"Lord, I can't tell others about Jesus. I am not good enough. I don't know the Bible well enough." We have all used that reasoning, and guess what? It doesn't hold up in His court of law. Moses tried it and look how well that worked out for him. God has been around the block a time or two with that argument. God's reply, "I have taken away your disgrace. I have covered it with the blood of My Son. I have deposited My Spirit into your soul. My Spirit is all the power you need, He will give you all the words you need to speak, and he will give you all the faith you will need for all situations."

"How kind the Lord is! He has taken away my disgrace!" Luke 1:25 NLT

"So this is how God acts to remedy my unfortunate condition!" Luke 1:25 Message Bible

"The Lord has done this for me! He has looked with favor in these days to take away my disgrace among the people" Luke 1:25 HCSB.

"I have lived with the disgrace of being barren for all these years. Now God has looked on me with favor. When I go out in public with my baby, I will not be disgraced any longer" Luke 1:25 The Voice Bible.

Hold your head up people! God has taken away our disgrace!

Questions to ponder and store in your heart:

What is it that God is calling you to do?

What is your argument that you place before God as to why you can't possibly do this thing He is asking you to do?
How has God taken away your disgrace?

How did God take away Elizabeth's disgrace?

How has God taken away your disgrace?

"Lord, thank you for taking away all my disgrace. Through the shed blood of Jesus my sins have been covered."

FROM A - Z

Day Eleven

"But the fruit of the Spirit is love, joy, peace, patience, kindness, goodness, faithfulness, gentleness, and self-control. Against such things there is no law" Galatians 5:22-23 NIV.

A few days later Mary hurried to the hill country of Judea, to the town where Zechariah lived. She entered the house and greeted Elizabeth. At the sound of Mary's greeting, Elizabeth's child leaped within her, and Elizabeth was filled with the Holy Spirit. Elizabeth gave a glad cry and exclaimed to Mary, "God has blessed you above all women, and your child is blessed. Why am I so honored, that the mother of my Lord should visit me? When I heard your greeting, the baby in my womb jumped for joy. You are blessed because you believed that the Lord would do what he said" Luke 1:39-45 NLT.

I wrote in my prayer journal, "Lord, make me into Elizabeth." The more I study this first woman of Christmas, the more I want to be like her. Actually, as I study each "Little Woman of Christmas" I want to be a hybrid of Elizabeth, Mary, and Anna. I want various characteristics from these women. Each has such treasures to offer.

You will see as we go through their lives during that first Christmas so long ago; but for now, I cannot leave Elizabeth. It is like she has pulled up a rocker; I am sitting at her feet, and all I see is this beautiful, quiet, humble, regal woman filled with the Holy Spirit of God. I recall the adjectives found in

Galatians 5:22-23. This verse lists the fruit of the Spirit. I see love, joy, peace, patience, kindness, goodness, faithfulness, gentleness, and self-control. Yes, yes, yes, check, check, check. Elizabeth was all those words. In my humble opinion, those words were her nouns. Elizabeth was love. Elizabeth was joy. Elizabeth was peace, patience, kindness, goodness, faithfulness, and gentleness.

I believe she was self-control, because only by exercising self-control would she have been able to go into seclusion for five months to celebrate privately all that the Lord has done for her. She closed up shop. She closed out friends. She did not need the companionship of the women who had questioned her barrenness for all those years. She shut herself off from all speculation and gossip. At this point her soul yearned for moments with God. She knew that to be in His Presence was fullness of joy. Only God gave her the affirmation and the confirmation she sought. So she became a hermit. She hibernated and nourished herself with the Bread of Life.

Today, the trait that jumps out at me is her sensitivity to what God was doing around her. She had an inner glow flow throughout her life, and it was not the glow of pregnancy. It was the glow of a righteous life before the Lord. Her righteous life produced the fruit of the Spirit.

The New Living Translation reads, "At the sound of Mary's greeting..." Instantaneously Elizabeth gave a glad cry and said something to the effect, "Mary you're with child and that child is the Son of God!"

WHAAAAAT? Did I miss a verse or two? Where was the part Mary told Elizabeth about Gabriel's visit? At what point did Mary tell Elizabeth she was with child? How did Elizabeth go from hearing Mary say "Hi" to declaring, "You're pregnant and you are the mother of my Lord?" Talk about jumping from

A to Z! The Son of God had recently entered her home and Elizabeth knew Emmanuel, who is God with us, was present so she worshipped. Now that is what I call being sensitive to the Spirit.

I love this scene. Elizabeth was six months pregnant. Her little baby bump was now a round belly. John would have been rolling across her stomach, and his fingers would have been wrapping around her ribs.

My daughter-in-law was recently pregnant. We heard the baby's heartbeat at around four months. Little Ezekiel hopped all over the place while he was tucked inside Whitney. When Whitney was six months pregnant, Ezekiel kicked and jockeyed for more stretching space. I remember when I was pregnant with Ezekiel's daddy. That boy kicked field goals inside my tummy for many months.

The verse says, "At the sound of Mary's greeting the baby leaped." Some versions translate the word "jumped." Whatever type of movement John did inside of Elizabeth at the moment she heard Mary's greeting was more than merely a kick. John, not yet out of Elizabeth's womb, leaped for joy! Truly I am awestruck at this whole scene. This is no ordinary meeting of two pregnant women and two unborn sons. When God is involved everything becomes EXTRA ORDINARY! Did Elizabeth remember Gabriel's promise? Her son "would be filled with the Holy Spirit while still in his mother's womb" Luke 1:15 HCSB.

The moment John leaped inside of her, Elizabeth was filled with the Holy Spirit. She began shouting and exclaiming, "You are the most blessed of women" Luke 1:42 HCSB.

"How could this happen to me, that the mother of my Lord should come to me?" Luke 1:43 HCSB This mother knew that her son was leaping for joy inside of her. "She who has believed is blessed because what was spoken to her by the LORD will be fulfilled!" Luke 1:45 HCSB

Not once did Mary tell her about Gabriel's visit. Not once did Mary have a chance to even speak. Elizabeth, who had been in seclusion for the last five months and had spoken very few words, now couldn't stop talking and rejoicing. That is what happens when you are filled with the Spirit of God.

Can you see why I want to be like Elizabeth? She knew God was always at work around her. She knew Emmanuel - God with us. She recognized God entering her world. She recognized Her Savior coming into her home.

God is at work all around me. He is still Emmanuel - God with us. He is present with me. I want to speak to a world of hurting people "God is here. He is at work! I know this!"

Questions to ponder and store in your heart:

John 3:5 NLT Jesus tells Nicodemus, "I assure you, no one can enter the Kingdom of God without being born of water and the Spirit." What does the Spirit of God allow us entrance into?

How do we gain the deposit of the Holy Spirit according to 2 Corinthians 5:5?

How can you be more sensitive to the fact that Jesus really is Emmanuel – God with us?

How amazing is this scene? How did John, who was not even born yet, recognize The Lord in his presence?

"Lord, make me sensitive to Your presence. Help me see Jesus everywhere I go."

From Insignificant to Significant From Ordinary to Extra-Ordinary

Day Twelve

"In the sixth month of Elizabeth's pregnancy, the angel Gabriel was sent by God to a town in Galilee called Nazareth, to a virgin engaged to a man named Joseph, of the house of David. The virgin's name was Mary. And the angel came to her and said, "Rejoice, favored woman! The Lord is with you" Luke 1:26-28 NET.

Now Philip was from Bethsaida, the town of Andrew and Peter. Philip found Nathanael and told him, "We have found the One Moses wrote about in the Law (and so did the prophets): Jesus the son of Joseph, from Nazareth!" "Can anything good come out of Nazareth?" Nathanael asked him" John 1:44-46 NET.

I wonder, what was going through Gabriel's mind as he approached the village of Nazareth? He was "on a mission" once again. The Lord God had summoned. You could feel the electricity of heaven these days. "The plan" was unfolding. The armies of heaven didn't know the whole plan but each angelic soldier and messenger angel stood at the ready to do all that "the maestro" orchestrated. This plan was of the utmost importance. With this plan, victory would be won for all of mankind. The excitement of heaven was palpable. It could hardly be contained. Gabriel knew the importance of completing his part in the "unfolding."

As this mighty Messenger Angel approached this insignificant farming village, did he hear the words, "God's ways are not our ways. His ways are higher than our ways?" The village of Nazareth was a small agricultural village. It had no trade routes. It was of little economic importance. In fact, it was located in Galilee, known to most as a heathen circle. Nazareth was in Palestine. A disciple of Jesus', Nathanael, would one day question how The Messiah could possibly come from Nazareth. "Can anything good come from there?" he asked his friend Philip.

Nazareth was an unknown village of little significance among the Jewish people and the Roman Empire; however, this village was the setting of an extraordinary encounter. It was in Nazareth that the Angel Gabriel intersected Mary's everyday ordinary life.

I would like to have known what Mary was doing when Gabriel showed up on her doorstep. Wouldn't you? Zechariah was in a sacred place when he met Gabriel, but Mary was in an ordinary, everyday occurrence doing an ordinary, everyday job. She was probably preparing for her wedding day. She was doing something she had been doing over and over since the day she became engaged to Joseph. An ordinary young betrothed peasant girl who was dreaming of her wedding day was about to learn her ordinary life was about to become extra-ordinary! An insignificant village in Galilee was about to become the significant hometown to our Savior, the

Lord Jesus Christ. The population of this village probably did not exceed 500. Every one knew every one. Insignificant becomes significant and ordinary was about to meet EXTRA-ORDINARY!

As I travel through these chapters of that first Christmas so long ago, I feel like Ebenezer Scrooge soaring back through time with the Ghost of Christmas past. Except, my travel guide is the Holy Spirit of God. Instead of trying to remove a humbug attitude, the Lord is igniting in me a deep love once again for the true reason for this season. I see in these first Christmas people a vision of who I want to become. Parts of their stories become parts of my story. Now, as I soar over this tiny insignificant agricultural village of Nazareth and look down at this young teenage peasant girl, I see myself reflected in the village lights. I have felt insignificant, usual, and ordinary. "Who am I to write and reflect on God's Word? I don't have a seminary doctorate abbreviation at the beginning of my name. Who am I to tell people about the Prince of Peace when I am a bundle of chaotic nerves, and worries, and fears?" I feel ordinary, but God has put EXTRA-ORDINARY inside of me. When I accepted Jesus as my Savior the Holy Spirit of God came in and took up residence in my heart.

Now as I soar above this tiny village in Galilee with the Holy Spirit of God, I see the God who turns insignificant into significant. I see God turning the usual into unusual. I see my ordinary become extra-ordinary. That's my God! That is what the whole of the First Christmas became. From the time Gabriel was sent on his first mission to the moment Wise Men and kings bowed down to worship the King of Kings who was wrapped up in a young child, God made ordinary EXTRA-ORDINARY.

Questions to ponder and store in your heart:

Look around you. What are you doing that seems ordinary to you?

Mary did not wake up that morning expecting to see Gabriel at her doorstep, but God entered in and changed her day. How can God change this ordinary day for you and make it EXTRA-ORDINARY?

What changes in your day would you have to make to have an EXTRA-ORDINARY day with God?

"Lord, with You there are no ordinary days. You have made me; therefore I am extraordinary."

A 'Steel Magnolia'

Day Thirteen

"In the sixth month of Elizabeth's pregnancy, the angel Gabriel was sent by God to a town in Galilee called Nazareth, to a virgin engaged to a man named Joseph, of the house of David. The virgin's name was Mary. And the angel came to her and said, "Rejoice, favored woman! The Lord is with you." But she was deeply troubled by this statement, wondering what kind of greeting this could be. Then the angel told her: "Do not be afraid, Mary for you have found favor with God" Luke 1:26-30 NET.

"But Mary treasured up all these things and pondered them in her heart" Luke 2:19 NIV.

"Then he went down to Nazareth with them and was obedient to them, but his mother treasured all these things in her heart" Luke 2:51NIV.

What can I, -- a mature woman of 54, married for 36 years, who has birthed three kids who are now fully grown with families of their own, a grandmother of 3, and a woman who has walked with the Lord for over forty years, -- what could I possibly learn from a young teenage girl who was still a virgin, not even married and had never ventured out into this great big world? What can I learn from a young peasant girl who had never even left her hometown of Nazareth? Well, let me tell you. This "worldly woman" of 54 can learn plenty

61

from this innocent child, especially how to live a pleasing life unto the Lord.

Mary joins a long list of people who have been set apart by God. The scriptures are full of men and women who God called by name and declared to all the righteous condition of their heart.

"This is the account of Noah and his family. Noah was a righteous man, the only blameless person living on earth at the time, and he walked in close fellowship with God" Genesis 6:9 NLT.

"After the birth of Methuselah, Enoch lived in close fellowship with God for another 300 years, and he had other sons and daughters. Enoch lived 365 years, walking in close fellowship with God. Then one day he disappeared, because God took him" Genesis 5:22-24 NLT.

Who is this young lady that God memorialized for all time? This is the woman God chose to be the mother of His One and Only Begotten Son, and she was hardly a woman. She had barely entered her teenage years.

"Therefore, the Lord Himself will give you a sign: The virgin will conceive, have a son, and name him Immanuel" Isaiah 7:14 HCSB.

Hundreds of years before Mary was born, God told Isaiah the prophet about her. God had Mary in His mind before even one day of Mary's life came to be. What type of woman was this that the Lord God would favor her so much? She was the type of young woman this older woman wants to emulate. I am first drawn to her heart condition. I believe it was the one trait that distinguished her from all her peers. She had a heart and mindset that wanted and received the blueprints of God.

Gabriel greeted her and said "You who are highly favored!" This is how I want to be known by God. "Highly

Favored!" with an exclamation mark. She was a recipient of God's grace. She did not bestow the favor, but it was God who gave it to her. She willingly received God's benefits. That was it. She had not worked to get God's favor but she had a heart that willingly accepted God's favor. Her heart was open. Her heart was genuine.

Mary's reaction intrigues me. The presence of this impressive messenger angel did not frighten her as Gabriel had done to Zechariah. "But she was greatly troubled by his words and began to wonder about the meaning of this greeting." It wasn't Gabriel's presence that confused her; it was the meaning of Gabriel's greeting that disturbed her. His salutation revolved in her mind. Mary had a pondering spirit. She was a greater thinker. She would meditate on things and search out true meanings. She was contemplative. I wonder why Gabriel's greeting frightened her and not his personification as was the case with Zechariah? Wouldn't his overpowering presence have cowered her? When the thin veil between heaven and earth was lifted and Mary saw this Mighty Angel of God, was that a normal episode for her? Had she been so sensitive to the heavenly beings that this manifestation did not bother her?

Paul tells us in Philippians 4:8 in the NIV, "Finally, brothers and sisters, whatever is true, whatever is noble, whatever is right, whatever is pure, whatever is lovely, whatever is admirable – if anything is excellent or praiseworthy – think about such things." Colossians 3:1-2 in the New English Translation tells us, "Therefore if you have been raised with Christ, keep seeking the things above where Christ is, seated at the right hand of God. Keep thinking about things above, not things on the earth."

Were these the things Mary stored in her thoughts? Was this appearance a norm for her because she fixed her mind on things of God and not of earth? It was the greeting that brought turmoil to her.

It was her contemplative heart and mind that draws me to her. King David had such a spirit about him. He once penned these words:

"At night I remember my music; I meditate in my mind and my spirit ponders" Psalm 77:6 HCSB.

Such was the spirit of this young girl. God chose this type of personality to be the mother of his Son. He chose someone who would treasure the events in Jesus' life and would hide them in her heart.

I call her a 'Steel Magnolia.' Yes, I name her after one of my favorite movies, but how befitting the name. She would need the strength of steel to trust the plan of God in her life. It would be this steel-like strength that would keep her planted at the foot of the cross as she watched her eldest brutally crucified. It was her meditations of God's commands that held her firmly planted as she watched her Son die a slow excruciating death, but it was her vulnerability and openness that caused her to store all these things in her heart; so I describe her as a magnolia. Mary had a heart totally open to the activity of God in her life. In the same way as a magnolia flower opens its petals wide, Mary laid her heart bare before God so that she could receive His Son no matter what may come. Mary was a paradox, a mix of strength and vulnerability.

That is the trait this older woman gleans from this younger woman. She had a heart that contemplated the Word of God, and a mind that pondered the activity of God. She was a mother who treasured the Son of God.

As I have already mentioned, I can unearth many treasures of God from the generations that surround me. I consider my oldest daughter one of my wisest advisors. I look at my middle child and see another contemplative spirit. I see the mighty man of God my youngest child has become. Yes, I can learn much from those who have gone before me, and I can learn much from those who are coming behind me.

And now I ponder and fix my thoughts on the things of God.

Questions to ponder and store in your heart:

How did Gabriel describe Mary?

What can you learn from Mary?

What are ways you can keep your mind fixed on things above and not on things of earth?

What are things you can learn from all the different generations that surround you?

"Lord, I fix my thoughts on things above. Give me a stable mind."

What's in a Name?

Day Fourteen

"But the angel reassured her saying, "Do not yield to your fear, Mary, for the Lord has found delight in you and has chose to surprise you with a wonderful gift. You will become pregnant with a baby boy, and you are to name him Jesus. He will be supreme and will be known as the Son of the Highest. And the Lord God will enthrone him as King on his ancestor David's throne. He will reign as King of Israel forever, and his reign will have no limit." Luke 1:30-33 The Passion Translation

We call Him Jesus. Ethiopians call Him, "Eyesus." The name of Jesus in Chinese is "Yesu," in Russian it is "Iisus," and in Spanish and French it is spelled Jesus but with different punctuation markings and different pronunciations. His name is Jesus. Mary was commanded to name Him Jesus, in Aramaic "Eashoa," and in Greek "Iisous." The name Jesus is a rendition of the Hebrew name "Yeshua." It is a form of Joshua, the great military hero of Israel. Joshua was the one who led the Israelites into the Promised Land after Moses' death. Joshua was a foreshadowing of the True Savior of Israel, Jesus. I look at all the names of Jesus in other languages and see how similar each is to another. His name is like no other name.

"As he considered this, and angel of the Lord appeared to him in a dream. "Joseph, son of David," The angel said, "Do not be afraid to take Mary as your wife. For the child within her was conceived by the Holy Spirit. And she will have a son, and you are to name him Jesus, for he will save his people from their sins." All of this occurred to fulfill the Lord's message through his prophet: "Look! The virgin will conceive a child! She will give birth to a son, and they will call him Immanuel, which means 'God is with us'" Matthew 1:20-23 NLT.

"All right then, the Lord himself will give you the sign. Look! The virgin will conceive a child! She will give birth to a son and will call him Immanuel (which means 'God is with us") Isaiah 7:14 NLT.

"Immanuel! God is with us!" Isaiah wrote these words about Jesus some seven hundred years before His birth. Can you imagine this faithful prophet sitting down to write and God giving him a picture into the future to see a day when He will come down and live among His creation. I am sure this treasured prophet's hands shook as he wrote those words down to be memorialized as a prophecy to the nation of Israel. Did he want to jump up and down and run outside to shout it from his rooftop? "God is going to come to you O Israel in the form of a human whom you all can see, touch, hear, and feel!" Those were not the only words Isaiah wrote about the coming "Promise."

"In the sixth month of Elizabeth's pregnancy, God sent the angel Gabriel to Nazareth, a village in Galilee, to a virgin named Mary. She was engaged to be married to a man named Joseph, a descendant of King David" Luke 1:26.

"For unto us a child is born, unto us a Son is given, and the government will be on his shoulders. And he will be called Wonderful Counselor, Mighty God, Everlasting Father, Prince of Peace. Of the greatness of his government and peace there will be no end. He will reign on David's throne and over his kingdom, establishing and upholding it with justice and righteousness from that time on and forever. The zeal of the Lord Almighty will accomplish this" Isaiah 9:6-7.

Wonderful Counselor!

Mighty God!

Everlasting Father!

Prince of Peace!

Isaiah also was told other names to give our Savior. These names for Isaiah weren't casual names holding no meaning. No, they were personal names. They were adjectives. These names described a different character of Jesus. Mighty God, spoke to Isaiah as a "Hero God." "Prince of Peace" was the one who would take the government on His shoulders and reign in peace and well being for all in His realm. Casual names, indeed not! Not for Isaiah. Not for us.

We call Jesus by many names. The Lord God calls Him "Son." The angel Gabriel spoke of Him as a "wonderful gift." Mary and Joseph were allowed to call Him son also. The prophet Jeremiah once named Him, "The Lord is Our Righteousness!"

"For the time is coming," says the Lord, "when I will raise up a righteous descendant from King David's line. He will be a King who rules with wisdom. He will do what is just and right throughout the land. And this will be his name: 'The Lord Is Our Righteousness.' In that day Judah will be saved and Israel will live in safety" Jeremiah 23:5-6 NLT.

John wrote in Revelation 19:16 NLT, "On his robe at his thigh was written this title: King of all Kings and Lord of all Lords."

Our Savior has been given many names. Each name is another facet of His character. Gabriel told Mary to name her Son "Jesus." The name means, "Jehovah is salvation." Gabriel and Isaiah both called Him "Immanuel" - which means "God with us." Every time I read that name I think of the scene in "Horton Hears a Who" and the people of Whoville start shouting "We are here! We are here! We are here!" In my head my thoughts go into repeat mode, "God is here! God is here! God is here!"

Israel was waiting on the one they called "Messiah." It means the anointed one or chosen one. Webster"s dictionary says, "Messiah - the promised deliverer of the Jewish nation." Some called Him "Jehovah Rapha" - "The Lord is my Healer. He is called "Elohim Shama: The God Who Hears." Jesus is that faithful friend who puts all else aside when we show up with a need. God gives us His undivided attention. He stoops to our level, locks His gaze on us, and He listens. How encouraging to know that in Christ, God is completely empathetic to our human struggles. Even when no one else seems to be paying attention, you can trust that God hears the cries of your heart.

I call Him my "Wonderful Counselor." Believe you me, I need a counselor for without Jesus I think I would have no sanity or clarity. I call Him "Mighty God." The mighty in this name literally means "Hero." "Jesus did you ever know that you are my Hero. You are everything I wish I could be!"

"Therefore God exalted him to the highest place and gave him the name that is above every name, that at the name of Jesus every knee should bow, in heaven and on earth and under the earth, and every tongue acknowledge that Jesus Christ is Lord, to the glory of God the Father" Philippians 2:9-11 NIV.

I asked, "What's in a name?" Paul wrote to the church at Philippi, "Jesus is the name that is above all names!" His name is who He is. His name is what He does! Jesus saves. There are many names because His character is multifaceted and He can do all things. What is your name for Jesus the Messiah?

Questions to ponder and store in your heart:

"Seth also had a son, and he named him Enosh. At that time people began to call on the name of the Lord." Genesis 4:26

The word "call" in Hebrew is "qara." It means to cry out, to shout or speak out. It means to proclaim. Qara often describes calling out loudly in an attempt to get someone's attention. Have you ever had a time when you needed to call out loudly to God and you felt like you had to get His attention? Describe that kind of gut wrenching trial.

What name of Jesus would you call out in your time of need?

Why not shout it out loud right now?

"Lord, I shout it out right now, "You are my Prince of Peace, and I need You."

The Shepherd's Candle
The Candle of Joy

The Third Sunday of Advent
Day Fifteen

Today is the third Sunday in the Advent Season. I light a pink candle. It is "The Shepherd's Candle" or the "Candle of Joy." Let's listen as the angels said, "Joy to the World."

"In those days a decree went out from Caesar Augustus that the whole empire should be registered. This first registration took place while Quirinius was governing Syria. So everyone went to be registered, each to his own town. And Joseph also went up from the town of Nazareth in Galilee, to Judea, to the city of David, which is called Bethlehem, because he was of the house and family line of David, to be registered along with Mary, who was engaged to him and was pregnant. While they were there, the time came for her to give birth. Then she gave birth to her firstborn Son, and she wrapped Him snugly in cloth and laid Him in a feeding trough — because there was no room for them at the lodging place.

In the same region, shepherds were staying out in the fields and keeping watch at night over their flock. Then an angel of the Lord stood before them, and the glory of the Lord shone around them, and they were terrified. But the angel said to them, "Don't be afraid, for look, I proclaim to you good news of great joy that will be for all the people: Today a

Savior, who is Messiah the Lord, was born for you in the city of David. This will be the sign for you: You will find a baby wrapped snugly in cloth and lying in a feeding trough." Suddenly there was a multitude of the heavenly host with the angel, praising God and saying: Glory to God in the highest heaven, and peace on earth to people He favors! When the angels had left them and returned to heaven, the shepherds said to one another,

"Let's go straight to Bethlehem and see what has happened, which the Lord has made known to us." They hurried off and found both Mary and Joseph, and the baby who was lying in the feeding trough.

After seeing them, they reported the message they were told about this child, and all who heard it were amazed at what the shepherds said to them. But Mary was treasuring up all these things in her heart and meditating on them. The shepherds returned, glorifying and praising God for all they had seen and heard, just as they had been told" Luke 2:1-20 HCSB.

Can't you imagine that night? "What a sight and what a sound that must have been." I can hardly read those verses without hearing Linus' voice in my head, "Poor Charlie Brown." He can get no respect. Charlie Brown is feeling those Christmas blue's. There is loneliness in his soul. "Isn't there somebody who can tell me what Christmas is all about?" Every time I watch the "Charlie Brown Christmas" I can feel Charlie's sadness. That is how touching that scene is for me, but then enter Linus stage right, "And there were in the same country shepherds abiding in the fields keeping watch over their sheep by night." Linus would start reading in his child's voice with a hint of a lisp, and as he recites this passage in Luke, the gloomy cloud over my heart begins to lift. Linus continues reading, "For unto you is born this day in the city of David a Savior which is Christ the Lord..." Then he walks back to Charlie Brown, "And that is what Christmas is all about Charlie Brown" Joy comes flooding back in!

So many surround us who really don't know what Christmas is all about. They hustle and bustle in search of that perfect gift. Store clerks work longer hours trying to appease hassled shoppers. Government buildings are banned from displaying nativity scenes. School children are given a "winter break" and no longer call it "Christmas break." Commercials entice us to buy more, or buy the most innovative new technology rolling out of the manufacturer's shelves. The Christmas season has become a harried holiday. Everyone rushes from one party to the next, and they wonder what is wrong. They wonder what they are missing during this time. They suffer from the "Christmas Blues." We focus on empty commercialism and things of this world. Those things cannot possibly fill that void. We are missing "Peace on Earth." We were made to celebrate God and when we don't worship; we tend to sing "The Blues." We will have a "Blue Christmas" without Christ at the center of it all. What will wipe out those "Christmas Blues?" We must remember what Christmas is all about!

My husband and I light Christmas Advent Candles because they help us remember the birth of our Savior. Today as Kevin and I light the pink "Shepherd's Candle" or the "Candle of Joy," we read Luke 2:1-20, and listen to "Joy to the World" and remember the night the dark sky lit up as the "Glory of the Lord" shone all around. We remember the night our Savior entered our world as a baby and we look forward to a day when the sky will roll back, a trumpet will sound, and our Savior will come back as King of Kings and Lord of Lords!

Questions to ponder and store in your heart:

God instructed Moses to set up special celebrations throughout the year. These celebrations served to remind the people of Israel of all that the Lord God had done to deliver Israel from their slavery in Egypt. What has the Lord done for you throughout your life?

Christmas can be a celebration to remember that God sent His One and Only Son into our world to free us from our bondage to sin. What has the Lord delivered you from recently that causes you to celebrate?

What special traditions do you practice that will help you remember the "True Reason for the Season?"

"Lord, I celebrate You. Help us as the family of God to pass down Your story to those who come behind us."

Overshadowed

Day Sixteen

"How will this be," Mary asked the angel, "since I am a virgin?" The angel answered, "The Holy Spirit will come on you, and the power of the Most High will overshadow you. So the holy one to be born will be called the Son of God" Luke 1:34-35 NIV.

"For no word from God will ever fail" Luke 1:37 NIV.

Gabriel told Mary how she would become pregnant even though she had known no man. He spoke these words, "The Holy Spirit will come on you, and the power of the Most High will overshadow you." God was literally about to cast his shadow over Mary. His shadow was going to envelop her. God's overshadowing presence always brings His plan to pass.

These Old Testament verses add a mental picture of what it looks like when God's Presence overshadows His people and His temple.

"And to the eyes of the sons of Israel the appearance of the glory of the LORD was like a consuming fire on the mountain top" Exodus 24:17 NAS.

"When Solomon had finished praying, the fire came down from heaven and consumed the burnt offering and the sacrifices, and the glory of the Lord filled the temple. The priests could not enter the temple of the LORD because the glory of the Lord had filled it" 2 Chronicles 7:1-2 NIV.

"And Moses was not able to enter the Tent of Meeting because the cloud remained upon, and the glory of the Lord filled the tabernacle" Exodus 40:35 NAS.

God's glory and His Overshadowing Presence take up space and volume. Think of filling a jar completely full with sand; now try stuffing a rock into that jar. That is what Moses experienced in Exodus 40:35. That tabernacle could not hold one more person because God's Glory took up all the space! The priests of the Lord could not enter the newly built Temple of God because His Presence filled every inch of that building! This was the Presence that was about to come upon Mary! Luke 1:35 says, "The power of the Most High will overshadow you..." The word power in the Greek is dynamis. Dynamite is formed from dynamis. Dynamis literally means "the ability to perform." God, who is the Only One who has the power to perform this act that Gabriel described, was about to cast His Overpowering Shadow upon Mary's womb! This act was an energy force greater than that of a nuclear explosion.

Mary had asked Gabriel, "How will this happen?" Gabriel explained it to her. Again, try to get your mind on that scene. Mary was wrapped up in that glorious cloud. I have to believe she felt it. I have to believe she knew the moment when the Son of God entered her. This verse is that Shekinah Glory of the Lord described in the verses above, the Shekinah Glory that took up so much space Moses and the priests couldn't enter into the structures.

Now even as I am imagining the moment that the power of the Most High overshadowed Mary, my throat is constricting, -- my heart feels as if it is overpowering my chest. Yes I have to believe Mary could feel the moment The Son of God entered her womb as an embryo. I have to believe it was a moment that couldn't be ignored. I have to believe she felt the Holy Spirit of God come upon her. What a day! What a moment! The God of all creation implanted His only Begotten Son into the womb of a young girl who had never known a man! At that moment could Father God already feel the absence of His Son who had sat enthroned with Him in the Heavens? God's loss was our gain. At that moment, The Son of God wrapped up all of His Glory and Majesty and Royalty in the form of an embryo. At that moment the King of Kings and the Lord of Lords traded in a throne for a womb. I have to believe the Cloud of Glory that overshadowed Mary at this moment was palpable. I have to believe it was visible. I have to believe it was a magical moment.

I have had that magical moment. I still remember it. I still remember asking Jesus to come and forgive me of my sins and live in my heart. I remember coming home from Sunday night church. There was a song resonating. "Fill my cup Lord. I lift it up Lord. "I still remember knowing I needed a Savior. It was a long time ago. I was eight. I still remember. It did feel good. I did feel the weight of God's Glory coming and filling my heart, but at the same moment it felt like a weight had been lifted off of me.

I challenge each of us to start praying this prayer starting with this Christmas season:

*"Lord fill me with Your Holy Spirit.Overshadow me as you did Mary so that I might love Jesus as You love Your Son."*I guarantee this is a prayer God desires to say yes to.

Questions to ponder and store in your heart:

How did Gabriel tell Mary she would conceive?

Describe the moment you asked Jesus to forgive you of your sins.

As you remember this moment, do you feel the weight of your sins being lifted from you, and being replaced with the weight of God's Son coming and taking up residence in your life?

If you have never experienced a moment like this, would you like to? Trust me, it is the most freeing moment you will ever experience. It will grant you eternal residence to live forever in God's Presence. Pray this prayer:

Lord God,
I believe you sent Your One and Only Son to this earth. I believe that He came, died on a cross, and rose again. I declare you, Jesus as Lord of my life. Please forgive me of my sins. In Jesus' name. Amen.

The bible says, "If we confess our sins, he is faithful and just and will forgive us our sins and purify us from all unrighteousness" 1 John 1:9 NIV.

And, "If you declare with your mouth, 'Jesus is Lord,' and believe in your heart that God raised him from the dead, you will be saved" Romans 10:9 NIV.

According to these verses, the moment you prayed that prayer, God forgave you. Your sins have been removed from you as far as the east is from the west. God's word is true. You have been forgiven. Though your sins are like scarlet they have been washed whiter than snow. The Holy Spirit of God has been deposited into your soul. God still implants His Son into our lives!

What's This Going to Cost Me?

Day Seventeen

"Gabriel appeared to her and said, "Greetings, favored woman! The Lord is with you!" Confused and disturbed, Mary tried to think what the angel could mean" Luke 1:28-29 NLT.

"Then Mary said, 'Behold I am the handmaiden of the Lord; let it be done to me according to what you have said.' And the angel left her" Luke 1:38 NKJV.

What did these words mean for Mary? These words spoken by Gabriel were about to drastically change the trajectory of Mary's life. No longer was she going to be a young maiden preparing for a grand wedding feast.

There were several steps in the Jewish marriage process at the time of Christ. According to the article, "Jewish Wedding Customs and the Bride of Messiah," the first step was known as the "Shiddukhin." This is the arrangement preliminary to the legal betrothal. It was common in ancient Israel for the father of the groom to select a bride for his son.

Luke 1:26-27 NIV says, "In the sixth month of Elizabeth's pregnancy, God sent the angel Gabriel to Nazareth, a village in Galilee, to a virgin named Mary. She was engaged to be married to a man named Joseph, a descendant of King David." Mary and Joseph had completed the "Shiddukhin." Joseph's father would have gone to Mary's father and the two men would have already entered into this preliminary step. The couple's fathers thought this was a good match.

Next, the two men would have had the "Ketubah," the marriage contract drawn up. In this contract, the groom promised to support his wife to be and the bride stipulated the contents of her dowry. The groom would then pay the "Mohar." It is a gift paid by the groom to the bride's family - but ultimately belongs to the bride. It changed her status and set her free from her parent's household.

The couple would then perform the "Mikveh," the ritual immersion. The bride and groom would separately take a ritual immersion. This immersion was prior to actually entering in to the formal betrothal period and was symbolic of spiritual cleansing. After the couple had individually undergone immersion, they would appear together under the "Huppah, a public canopy where they would express their intention of engagement. The wedding canopy was a symbol of a new household being formed.

After the ceremony, the couple was considered to have entered into the betrothal agreement. This period was to last for one year. During this time the couple was considered married - yet did not have sexual relations - and continued to live separately until the end of the betrothal. After the ceremony the groom would return to his home to focus on preparing a new dwelling place for his wife. Before his departure, he would give his wife a gift, the bridal gift. It was a pledge of his love for her. Its purpose was to be a reminder to his bride during their days of separation of his love for her, that he was thinking of her, and that he would return to receive her as his wife. During this betrothal time, the wife was to keep herself busy in preparation for the wedding day – specifically, wedding garments were to be sewn and prepared.

This is the period that Gabriel intersects Mary's life. She and Joseph are in their time of sanctification. They were to set aside and prepare themselves to enter into the covenant of marriage. This betrothal period was so binding that the couple would need a religious divorce to annul the contract. This option was only available to the husband, as the wife had no say in any divorce proceeding. The final step in the wedding process was the "Nissan," which means, "to carry." This is a graphic description - as the bride would be waiting for her groom to come - to carry her off to her new home. The bride took the betrothal seriously. The period of betrothal was a time of great expectation.

Enter Gabriel. He was bearing news that would change all these expectations for Mary. She would have been looking forward to the day Joseph would carry her off to her new home. She lived in a small town. Everyone was waiting in high anticipation for Mary and Joseph's wedding day. Was Mary sewing on her wedding garments this day as Gabriel greeted her?

No wonder she was confused and disturbed at Gabriel's greeting. She did contemplate what these words would mean for her life. When the announcement came that she would be with child before her actual wedding date, did she picture herself being drug to the city gates while her friends and family hurled large stones at her? For that was the punishment of an adulterer, stoning till death. But you know what? I never see the verse where Mary asks, "What's this going to cost me?" Actually the verse reads, "Mary responded, "I am the Lord's servant. May everything you have said about me come true." Luke 1:38. With that statement, gone was the big fancy wedding day where Joseph would sweep her away. She never even asks the question, "Lord how are you going to take care of me?" No, "May your word to me be fulfilled," was her answer. The Passion Bible says, "This is amazing! I will be a mother for the Lord!" I am thankful Mary didn't even consider, "What's this going to cost me?"

God's assignments come with a high price attached to them. Consider all that Jesus endured on His way to the cross. In Hebrews 12:2 Jesus inspired the writer to tell us to "fix our eyes on Jesus, the pioneer and perfector of faith. For the joy set before him he endured the cross, scorning its shame, and sat down at the right hand of the throne of God." The blessing that flows to us from our obedience far outweighs the cost of our obedience. If you don't believe me, ask some great heroes of our faith.

Ask Mary the mother of our Lord. Mary considered that the blessing she received from the Lord far outweighed the risk she was taking when she said yes. Consider her words a few verses later found in the Passion Translation. "My soul is ecstatic, overflowing with praises to God. My spirit bursts with joy over my life-giving God!" "From here on, everyone will know that I have been favored and blessed" Luke 1:46-47 Passion Translation.

Ask Paul. He was beaten, imprisoned, scorned and ridiculed but still he said, "For me to live is Christ, to die is gain."

Ask John. He was exiled to the Isle of Patmos for his belief in Jesus. While on that island, God gave him a revelation to show his servants what must soon take place.

These are the things I wish to take away from a young peasant girl from Nazareth: Her total obedience in the face of grave consequences. I want to live like that.

Questions to ponder and store in your heart:

How brave was Mary when she said, "May it be to me as you have said?"

There is always a cost when you decide to follow Jesus. Jesus tells us this in Luke. "But don't begin until you count the cost. For who would begin construction of a building without first calculating the cost to see if there is enough money to finish it?" Luke 14:28 NLT.

What is God calling you to do?

What is the cost?

What is the blessing of obedience?

Does the blessing outweigh the cost?

"Lord, I want to abandon my will and exchange it for Yours."

Are We There Yet?

Day Eighteen

"And consider your relative Elizabeth — even she has conceived a son in her old age, and this is the sixth month for her who was called childless. For nothing will be impossible with God." "I am the Lord's slave," said Mary. "May it be done to me according to your word." Then the angel left her. In those days Mary set out and hurried to a town in the hill country of Judah where she entered Zechariah's house and greeted Elizabeth"Luke 1:36-40 HCSB.

Gabriel has finished explaining to Mary about this supernatural pregnancy. Actually, I would call it jaw dropping. Just when Gabriel leaves us with mouths gaping over how Mary became pregnant, he inserts an "Oh by the way" at the end of this breathtaking event.

The New Living Translation says, "What's more, your relative Elizabeth has become pregnant in her old age! People used to say she was barren, but she has conceived a son and is now in her sixth month."

Amplified Version says, "Listen!"

Do those two statements seem random to you? Really, Gabriel? At the end of this exclamation point of Mary becoming pregnant with the Son of God you add a "what's more." I think that is why I have always missed these two statements of Gabriel's. They seem so anticlimactic. Even the word anticlimactic seems like an understatement to me. I don't get the reasoning behind them. Or I didn't until I watched the movie "Heaven is for Real." That movie is what helped me notice these verses. In the movie, the little boy would say random things about heaven after he had a near death experience. Everyone, including his dad, didn't quite know what to think of such proclamations by the little boy. Even his mom was skeptical. And let me tell you, moms are usually the first to be in their child's corner; however, this time, it was the dad who first believed.

This movie made me realize that this is what Mary, Zechariah, and Elizabeth all were facing. Each had been touched by heaven. Don't you know they wanted to tell everyone? Obviously Zechariah couldn't, seeing has how the angel made him mute. But Mary was overjoyed, and perplexed. She needed a sounding board. In our day, she would have tweeted all about it, but for one minor problem of being stoned to death. She was betrothed to be married to Joseph. It was set in stone. In the eyes of Israel she was already married. By Levitical law, if her husband had found out on their wedding night that his bride was not a virgin, that was grounds for stoning. It was hard enough for a young teenage girl to go home to her parents and say, "O yeah, mom and dad I am pregnant." By law, her village would have dragged her out to the towns square and everyone would have picked up stones. Read John 8. Mary's own fiancé had plans to send her and this unwanted pregnancy away. What was Mary to do? She was about to explode with this Good News.

Now do you get it? Now do you see the reasoning behind Gabriel's "What's More?" *I get it now.* God was protecting His Child and His Favored one. He was giving her a place to go. Someone with skin on that she could talk to about this blessed event. These weren't some random statements made by Gabriel; they had reasoning behind them.

The "how" of this plan had only briefly been laid out before Mary. She didn't balk, she didn't question, she just said, "Let it be done to me as you have said." Look at her next action, "With haste Mary went to the hill country to a town in Judah." I had to look that up. The Greek use the noun "spoude" which can carry the idea of eagerness, diligence enthusiasm, and zeal. Mary is in a hurry to leave, - that much is clear.

Think of it. She is young. Most bible scholars put her age between 12-14 and no older. Heaven had just touched earth and she was to play a major role in the "Plan of Salvation for all of mankind!" Adrenaline had to be flowing. The bible doesn't tell us if she went and got her parents permission. I looked this up. She, this young child, got ready and immediately after hearing she would bear the Son of God, she up and left her home in Nazareth. I don't know the time frame here, but at some point between the time Gabriel gave her the message and the time she left, the Holy Spirit of God, - the Power of the Most High, came down, overshadowed her, and implanted in her our Lord Jesus. As Max Lucado puts it, "A conception of Divine Grace with human disgrace" occurred. A most spectacular event happened in Mary's womb so she made haste to get out of Dodge so she could explain this to people who would understand her.

This young peasant girl had to be feeling pretty overwhelmed. She was in need of steadying and guidance. This whole experience had to have been so exciting. Now she was on an adventure. Her pregnancy begins with an arduous journey and will end with an arduous journey. Her path from Nazareth to the hill country of Judah covered between 80 and 100 miles. We don't know how she traveled or whom she traveled with. She was a poor peasant girl traveling through mountain passes and rocky terrain. I do not think she rode a horse. I don't think she would have had that kind of money. If she went on foot she could probably travel 20 miles a day. In addition, the Judean countryside was plagued by bandits and robbers. A young girl traveling alone would have been prime prey.

I picture her traveling in a caravan. Either way, it would have taken at least 4 or 5 days to travel to Elizabeth's house. Did she ever ask the question of every young child on a road trip, "Are we there yet?" On this journey she determinedly went, because God was sending Mary to Elizabeth and Zechariah, - other people who had been touched by God. People who would know exactly what she was experiencing. We need these types of people in our lives also. God knows we need them. I have a writing friend who recently published her first book, "Perfectly Weak." She is my pastor's wife, Casey Boyd. Again, God's Word has become real life for us. We are Elizabeth and Mary. (We aren't pregnant! I for one say Hallelujah to that!) But God definitely had our writing lives intersect. We have each other to walk alongside as we start this journey of writing together. We get each other. Each of us knows the fear of putting ourselves out there. We know the feeling of being vulnerable for the world to witness. We call each other and sound off and encourage one another to keep going no matter what because God has called us to this mission.

I think I am slow witted when it comes to understanding the ways of God, and the little implications He sends me everyday. Like I said it has taken me these many years to see these verses.

Look at verse 39. How long did it take Mary to grasp Gabriel's implication? She immediately leaves for Elizabeth's house.

"Elizabeth gave a glad cry and exclaimed to Mary, "God has blessed you above all women, and your child is blessed. Why am I so honored, that the mother of my Lord should visit me? When I heard your greeting, the baby in my womb jumped for joy" Luke 1:42-44 NLT.

In these words, Elizabeth affirmed for Mary the mission she was on. I know Mary knew she was carrying the Son of God, but she was barely pregnant. No way would she have felt baby Jesus stirring inside of her. Elizabeth's words here had to have been a balm to her soul. "Okay. Yeah all this did actually happen to me. I am on the right track."

Elizabeth gave Mary words of confirmation and affirmation. We all need those words. Words spoken to us to say, "You are on God's path for your life."

Like I said, Mary was thoughtful. She took everything to heart. Talked little and thought much. These types of people are very sensitive to those gentle nudges of the Holy Spirit.

Can you hear those nudges? Can you feel them? Is God planting a task, a mission, way down in the depths of your heart? Can you feel it coming together? Can you see the plan? What is God birthing in you?

The journey ahead may be filled with mountains and rocky terrain, but I guarantee each mission God calls you to, He will take care of you! He will give you someone to walk alongside of you to guide you and to work with you in this endeavor! In every mission from God you will have the guidance and power of the Holy Spirit to enable you!

Oh Hallelujah and thank you God!

Questions to ponder and store in your heart:

After saying the words, "I am the Lord's servant. May your word to me be fulfilled." What was Mary's first plan of action?

Put yourself in her shoes. What would you be feeling?

What mission or assignment is God birthing in you right now?

Look around. Who has God placed in your life to walk alongside of you on this assignment?

I guarantee God will place people in your life that will confirm and affirm this assignment He has given you. Go to that person and listen for God-given wisdom.

"Lord, You have a mission for me. Open my eyes to see all the people you have placed in my life. Help me listen to them and help me listen for Your wisdom."

The Holy Spirit of God

Day Nineteen

"The angel replied to her: "The Holy Spirit will come upon you, and the power of the Most High will overshadow you. Therefore, the holy One to be born will be called the Son of God" Luke 1:35 HCSB.

I would be remiss if I didn't take a good look at the most prominent figure in the Christmas story. He is the leading character. He is more of a presence than either you or I. "The Holy Spirit will come upon you." The Holy Spirit of God was the agent that came upon Mary and she became pregnant. The Holy Sprit of God was intricate in this First Christmas magic. The Holy Spirit of God was intricate in the magic of Creation.

"Now the earth was formless and empty, darkness covered the surface of the watery depths, and the Spirit of God was hovering over the surface of the waters" Genesis 1:2 HCSB.

Jesus is the Son of God. The Holy Spirit is the power of God. The Holy Spirit at work in our lives will always cause us to bring glory to the Son of God.

Jesus says of The Holy Spirit, "When the Counselor comes, the One I will send to you from the Father — the Spirit of truth who proceeds from the Father — He will testify about Me" John 15:26 HCSB.

How many times have we seen The Holy Spirit in action thus far in that first Christmas?

"When Elizabeth heard Mary's greeting, the baby leaped inside her, and Elizabeth was filled with the Holy Spirit" Luke 1:41 HCSB.

Then his father Zechariah was filled with the Holy Spirit and prophesied" Luke 1:67 HCSB.

I kept my grandsons once because their parents were leaving for a short vacation getaway. My daughter left small gifts for each of the boys. The boys were to open one gift a day while their parents were away. When they ran out of gifts the boys knew that is the day their parents returned. It helped with their separation anxiety.

As Jesus drew near to the time of His imminent departure; He tried to prepare his disciples. He could feel their anxiety as he explained his exit. He promised them a gift also. It was the gift of the Holy Spirit whom He would send to them after He departed from them. I present to you those promises and the ministry of the Holy Spirit.

"But very truly I tell you, it is for your good that I am going away. Unless I go away, the Advocate will not come to you; but if I go, I will send him to you. When he comes, he will prove the world to be in the wrong about sin and righteousness and judgment" John 16:7-8 NIV.

"But you will receive power when the Holy Spirit has come on you, and you will be My witnesses in Jerusalem, in all Judea and Samaria, and to the ends of the earth" Acts 1:8 HCSB.

"On the day of Pentecost all the believers were meeting together in one place. Suddenly, there was a sound from heaven like the roaring of a mighty windstorm, and it filled the house where they were sitting. Then, what looked like flames or tongues of fire appeared and settled on each of them. And everyone present was filled with the Holy Spirit and began speaking in other languages, as the Holy Spirit gave them this ability" Acts 2:1-4 NLT.

"Now the one who has fashioned us for this very purpose is God, who has given us the Spirit as a deposit, guaranteeing what is to come" 2 Corinthians 5:5 NIV.

"While Peter was still speaking these words, the Holy Spirit came on all who heard the message" Acts 10:44 NIV.

"For the Holy Spirit will teach you at that time what you should say" Luke 12:12 NIV.

I could go on and on with verse after verse of how the Holy Spirit of God manifests itself in our lives. We cannot do this Christian life without the Spirit of God alive and active in us. When our lives bring Glory to the Son of God, it is evident the Spirit of God is at work in us. The Holy Spirit of God will always implant Jesus into our hearts as he planted Jesus into Mary's womb.

The Holy Spirit of God who is alive and vibrant in our lives causes us to worship as Mary did.

"Mary responded, "Oh, how my soul praises the Lord. How my spirit rejoices in God my Savior! For he took notice of his lowly servant girl, and from now on all generations will call me blessed. For the Mighty One is holy, and he has done great things for me. He shows mercy from generation to generation to all who fear him. His mighty arm has done tremendous things! He has scattered the proud and haughty ones. He has brought down princes from their thrones and exalted the humble. He has filled the hungry with good things and sent the rich away with empty hands. He has helped his servant Israel and remembered to be merciful. For he made this promise to our ancestors, to Abraham and his children forever" Luke 1:46-55 NLT.

The Psalmist wrote, "Where can I go from your Spirit? Where can I flee from your presence? If I go up to the heavens, you are there; if I make my bed in the depths, you are there. If I rise on the wings of the dawn, if I settle on the far side of the sea, even there your hand will guide me, your right hand will hold me fast. If I say, "Surely the darkness will hide me and the light become night around me," even the darkness will not be dark to you; the night will shine like the day, for darkness is as light to you" Psalm 139:7-12 NIV.

When I look in the mirror, all I see is my reflection. So I repeat to myself this truth, "I am the temple and dwelling place of the Holy Spirit of God!"

Questions to ponder and store in your heart:

What evidence can you see of the Spirit's work in your life?
Do you worship God for all He has done in your life?

"But the fruit of the Spirit is love, joy, peace, forbearance, kindness, goodness, faithfulness, gentleness and self-control. Against such things there is no law" Galatians 5:22-23 NIV.

Are these traits flowing from your life no matter the circumstances?

These characteristics are like a check list for those who accept Jesus as our Savior. Only the Holy Spirit of God can produce these traits in us!

"Lord, fill my cup. I lift it up. Lord, fill me with Your Spirit and may others see Your fruit in me."

The Joys of Having a Baby

Day Twenty

"When it was time for Elizabeth's baby to be born, she gave birth to a son. And when her neighbors and relatives heard that the Lord had been very merciful to her, everyone rejoiced with her. When the baby was eight days old, they all came for the circumcision ceremony. They wanted to name him Zechariah, after his father. But Elizabeth said, "No! His name is John!" "What?" they exclaimed. "There is no one in all your family by that name." So they used gestures to ask the baby's father what he wanted to name him.

He motioned for a writing tablet, and to everyone's surprise he wrote, "His name is John." Instantly Zechariah could speak again, and he began praising God. Awe fell upon the whole neighborhood, and the news of what had happened spread throughout the Judean hills. Everyone who heard about it reflected on these events and asked, "What will this child turn out to be?" For the hand of the Lord was surely upon him in a special way.

Then his father, Zechariah, was filled with the Holy Spirit and gave this prophecy: "Praise the Lord, the God of Israel, because he has visited and redeemed his people. He has sent us a mighty Savior from the royal line of his servant David, as he promised through his holy prophets long ago. Now we will be saved from our enemies and from all who hate us. He has been merciful to our ancestors by remembering his sacred covenant— the covenant he swore with an oath to our ancestor Abraham. We have been rescued from our enemies so we can serve God without fear, in holiness and righteousness for as long as we live.

"And you, my little son, will be called the prophet of the Most High, because you will prepare the way for the Lord. You will tell his people how to find salvation through forgiveness of their sins. Because of God's tender mercy, the morning light from heaven is about to break upon us, to give light to those who sit in darkness and in the shadow of death, and to guide us to the path of peace." John grew up and became strong in spirit. And he lived in the wilderness until he began his public ministry to Israel" Luke 1:57-80 NLT.

At this point in the story, Mary was three months pregnant. Jesus was growing inside her. My daughter-in-law will tell you the baby was the size of an orange. She is keeping up with these things these days. According to Whitney's research, Jesus' eyes and fingers and toes were becoming distinct. If they had sonograms in those days, Mary could have seen the hand of God being formed inside her. I got to see pictures of my new grandchild this weekend. I saw the head and the arms. I think the baby was waving. The pictures were taken when Whitney was around three months pregnant. I think about those pictures as I write. This is what Jesus did for us! The One who walked on streets of gold, wrapped up His majesty and glory into a vulnerable innocent baby and placed Himself inside a young peasant girl's womb for nine months. God became one of us so we could become a child of His. That blows my mind. Whitney was still running five miles a couple of times a week when she was three months pregnant. That first Christmas, Mary packed up and traveled the same arduous journey back to her home in Nazareth, through valleys and hills, past bandits and thieves, she traveled the 100 or so miles on foot while carrying the Son of God in her womb. She was a courageous woman. No wonder God chose her!

Back in the hillsides of Judah, Mary's cousin Elizabeth was experiencing the pains of childbirth. She gave birth to a son as the Lord had promised her husband Zechariah. It was cause for celebration. The cousins and relatives, family and friends, neighbors and villagers, all came out to celebrate with Elizabeth and Zechariah. They were festive because they had heard that the Lord had shown great mercy on her. They came to rejoice with her. We rejoice over the blessings of God. All were gathered on the eighth day of this baby's life.

"Then God said to Abraham, "Your responsibility is to obey the terms of the covenant. You and all your descendants have this continual responsibility. This is the covenant that you and your descendants must keep: Each male among you must be circumcised. You must cut off the flesh of your foreskin as a sign of the covenant between you and Me. From generation to generation, every male child must be circumcised on the eighth day after his birth" Genesis 17:9-12 NLT.

This was that day. Elderly Elizabeth and voiceless Zechariah are gathered to honor the generational command God gave Abraham in Genesis 17.

The verse "I will always be your God and the God of your descendants after you. And I will give the entire land of Canaan, where you now live as a foreigner, to you and your descendants. It will be their possession forever, and I will be their God" Genesis 17:7-8 NLT.

Thousands of years earlier, the Lord God appeared to their ancestor Abraham, who at that time was named Abram.

God revealed to Abram that He is "El Shaddai - God Almighty." God told Abram, "Nothing is too hard for Me!" On that day, God changed Abram's name to Abraham, -- from "Exalted Father" to "Father of many." The Lord God Almighty made a covenant with Abraham on that day so long ago. The Only One who can keep a covenant, made an unbreakable covenant to father Abraham. It was an everlasting covenant. This was God's part of the covenant: "I will always be your God and the God of your descendants after you. And I will give the entire land of Canaan, where you now live as a foreigner, to you and your descendants. It will be their possession forever, and I will be their God." God made this unbreakable promise to an old man who had no descendants. He still told Abraham, "I am God Almighty and nothing is too hard for me!"

A covenant refers to two or more parties bound together. Usually a covenant is made between two equal parties, but this was not the case with this covenant between Abraham and God. God initiated this covenant. He determined the elements, and He was the One who confirmed this covenant. He was the One with the covenant keeping power. He signed this covenant with His name "El Shaddai." The only mark required by Abraham was circumcision. The ritual act of circumcision was done on the eighth day of the male child's life.

This was that day for the son of Zechariah and Elizabeth. All have gathered; the knife is laid out; the age-old ceremony begins. The baby boy's foreskin is removed while all are watching. I can't tell you what it would be like to watch a knife being taken to my son because Landry was taken from me at three days and the doctors surgically performed this procedure. He was brought back to me with his chin quivering and tears still in his eyes -- and I cried.

Elizabeth's heart had to have broken as she heard her baby cry, but circumcision was part of Abraham's covenant. It was a ceremony performed for every male descendant. It was their way to honor the covenant. Elizabeth would have stood stoic beside her husband. Zechariah and Elizabeth were both righteous before God. And because of their righteousness and faithfulness to El Shaddai, they didn't yield to peer pressure. I don't get why the crowd thought they had a right in naming Elizabeth's and Zechariah's baby, but that is exactly what this group had in mind. They were intending to call him Zechariah after his father! But this faithful couple didn't bend; they didn't yield. They held their ground and obeyed God in the face of peer pressure.

"No! His name is John." Elizabeth told them with an exclamation point. The gathering must have thought that name came from left field, but little did they know the name came from the heavenly field. They turned to Zechariah. Poor old Zack, still lived in the "Sound of Silence." Even his hearing was nonexistent for they had to use gestures to find out the baby's name. This scene had to have looked like the game of charades... "first word..." Can't you picture how ridiculous this crowd must have looked trying to act out how the couple must name this child after his father? What would these gestures look like? I have to believe God was up in heaven having a good ole time watching this parody being played out before Him. Was he sitting at the edge of His throne saying, "Wait for it! Wait for it!" as Zechariah was gesturing for a writing tablet? When he wrote, "His name is John," the world of silence was broken for Zechariah. At once his mouth was opened and his tongue was loosed! For the first time in nine months, Zechariah could speak; Zechariah could hear! El Shaddai - God Almighty had kept His promise once again!

101

Zechariah and Elizabeth had a choice to make: Obey or yield to peer pressure. They chose obedience. What they got in return was blessing for there is always God's blessing in our obedience.

"And at once Zachariah's mouth was opened and his tongue loosed, and he began to speak, blessing and praising and thanking God. And awe and reverential fear came on all their neighbors; and all these things were discussed throughout the hill country of Judea. And all who heard them laid them up in their hearts, saying, "Whatever will this little boy be then? For the hand of the Lord was so evidently with him protecting and aiding him." Now Zechariah his father was filled with and controlled by the Holy Spirit and he prophesied..." Luke 1:63-67 AMP.

"And the little boy grew and became strong in spirit..." Luke 1:80 AMP.

Elizabeth and Zachariah's obedience tipped the chalice of God's blessing. God had poured out the covenant blessing onto Father Abraham for his obedience and a whole nation was favored. As God poured out the blessing onto Elizabeth and Zachariah for their obedience, a whole village was favored as the wine of blessing was sloshed onto them. For that is how God's blessing rolls. When his people decide to obey, the blessing of obedience splashes onto all around.

Peer pressure or obedience. You weigh the scales. El Shaddai has the blessings at the ready to be poured onto to all. We simply have to choose to obey.

Questions to ponder and store in your heart:

Have you ever yielded to peer pressure?

What was the outcome?

What are you struggling with in your obedience to God?

What are the blessings you will receive in your obedience?

Write them down and keep them before you as you struggle.

"Lord, make me obedient to You. I humbly bow to Your commands."

Filled and Overflowing

Day Twenty One

Christmas is right around the corner. This week I will be full and overflowing with Christmas ham, turkey, dressing, and mashed potatoes. Yes, I am salivating, but being full and over stuffed in my stomach is not the full and overflowing I am talking about.

"Now Zachariah his father was filled with and controlled by the Holy Spirit and prophesied, saying, Blessed (praised and extolled and thanked) be the Lord, the God of Israel, because He has come and brought deliverance and redemption to His people! And He has raised up a Horn of salvation [a mighty and valiant Helper, the Author of salvation] for us in the house of David His servant– This is as He promised by the mouth of His holy prophets from the most ancient times [in the memory of man]– That we should have deliverance and be saved from our enemies and from the hand of all who detest and pursue us with hatred; To make true and show the mercy and compassion and kindness [promised] to our forefathers and to remember and carry out His holy covenant [to bless, which is all the more sacred because it is made by God Himself],

That covenant He sealed by oath to our forefather Abraham: To grant us that we, being delivered from the hand of our foes, might serve Him fearlessly In holiness (divine consecration) and righteousness [in accordance with the everlasting principles of right] within His presence all the days of our lives. And you, little one, shall be called a prophet of the Most High; for you shall go on before the face of the Lord to make ready His ways; to bring and give the knowledge of salvation to His people in the forgiveness and remission of their sins. Because of and through the heart of tender mercy and loving-kindness of our God, a Light from on high will dawn upon us and visit [us]. To shine upon and give light to those who sit in darkness and in the shadow of death, to direct and guide our feet in a straight line into the way of peace" Luke 1:67-79 AMP.

What does a person do when he is filled and overflowing with the Spirit of the Holy God? Well, that person doesn't moan and groan and rub their bellies while complaining that their self-indulgence led to gluttony. A spirit filled person does what Zechariah did! A life controlled by the Holy Spirit of God sees as God sees, thinks as God thinks, speaks only what God says to speak, and worships as one who is so thankful for all that God has done. The Holy Spirit of God saturates every thought and idea of one who is filled and overflowing with the Spirit. The Holy Spirit of God always glorifies the Son of God. A life filled by the Holy Spirit of God will always glorify the Son of God. A spirit filled life will speak with the creativity of God!

Zechariah was filled with the Holy Spirit of God. God's creative juices were flowing through him and so Zechariah composed and sang a worship song with these verses. The song is called the "Benedictus." There is amazing Hebrew poetry contained in this passage. The names of John, Zechariah, and Elizabeth are all found in this song. "He has shown us mercy" or "God's gracious gift" is found in the name John. Zechariah's name means, "God has remembered."

Elizabeth's name means, "God's Holy Covenant" or "Covenant Keeper."

Filled and overflowing with God's Spirit, Zechariah sees the Lord God as He really is, Our Hero-God! Our Hero-God came to set us free from the desecration of our sin. I feel like I need an exclamation point after each sentence. Zechariah, filled with God's Spirit, saw the truth of what God was doing. The Son of God was yet an embryo in Mary's womb, but Zechariah knew, with the birth of Jesus, God was paying the compensation of all of our faults. He also knew God looks at us through Grace colored sunglasses. He speaks of the tiny fetus growing in Mary and saw in that vulnerable state "A Horn of Salvation for Israel." Jesus would become our mighty and valiant helper. With the babe wrapped in Mary's womb, and living in Nazareth, our Covenant keeping God was fulfilling His promise to Father Abraham. Then Spirit-filled Zachariah took his own son in his arms and spoke over John all that he would one day become. A forerunner to Salvation, one who would one day turn the hearts of Israel back to God! Zechariah saw as the prophets of old foresaw:

"To give his people the knowledge of salvation through the forgiveness of their sins, because of the tender mercy of our God, by which the rising sun will come to us from heaven to shine on those living in darkness and in the shadow of death, to guide our feet into the path of peace" Luke 1:77-79 NIV.

Zechariah saw "The Light" that will dawn breaking open our darkness." That, my friends, is what a person filled and overflowing with the Spirit of God does. They see as God sees. They speak life and a future into people. I want to live like that!

Questions to ponder and store in your heart:

Obedience to God is key to being filled with the Holy Spirit. What does a Spirit filled life mean to you?

How do you think Zachariah could speak such truth? What did he describe about Jesus?

Zechariah described Jesus though Jesus was still in Mary's womb. How can you describe Jesus even though you have never physically touched Him?

"Lord, such wisdom can only come from above. I want to obey You. I want to speak words of life to all around me."

The Angel Candle
The Candle of Love

The Fourth Sunday of Advent
Day Twenty Two

"And there were shepherds living out in the fields nearby, keeping watch over their flocks at night. An angel of the Lord appeared to them, and the glory of the Lord shone around them, and they were terrified. But the angel said to them, "Do not be afraid. I bring you good news that will cause great joy for all the people. Today in the town of David a Savior has been born to you; he is the Messiah, the Lord. This will be a sign to you: You will find a baby wrapped in cloths and lying in a manger." Suddenly a great company of the heavenly host appeared with the angel, praising God and saying, "Glory to God in the highest heaven, and on earth peace to those on whom his favor rests" Luke 2:8-14 NIV.

"For God so loved the world that he gave his one and only Son, that whoever believes in him shall not perish but have eternal life" John 3:16 NIV.

"We love because he first loved us"1 John 4:19 NIV.

God's love for us is the reason that we had the first Christmas so long ago. There are days I tend to question the love of God, " Lord, if you really loved me, why aren't You answering this prayer?" Teresa of Avila, a sixteenth-century nun, once quipped, "If this is how you treat your friend, no wonder you have so few of them." This statement was not directed at a human companion but at the Lord himself. She uttered this right after being dumped in the mud when her cart overturned during a journey she had taken for the Lord. As I read that quote, I thought to myself, "I know how you feel, sister!" When bad things happen, I do have a tendency to blame God and wonder what I have done to make Him angry. Haven't you ever felt that frustration with God when your life wasn't going the way you planned? Especially when you think you are doing "your best" to serve Him. "What is it Lord? Haven't I worked hard enough for you?" The thing is, Romans 8 tells me, "nothing can separate me from the Love of God which is in Christ Jesus our Lord." We can't do enough to earn the Lord's favor! Not compared to all He has done for us! We all stand in the shadow of the cross. The blood and the torture of Jesus will always remain in the backdrop of our lives.

Today, Kevin and I light the fourth candle of Advent. It is the "Angel Candle" or "The Candle of Love." It reminds me that no matter what my circumstances, no matter how trying my struggles are, God Loves Me! He gave his one and only Son to die a terrible, horrific, bloody death on a torturous Roman cross. I need only to lay this scene over any and all of my trials, and that overlay will spell out God's love for me. That overlay will spell out God's love for you and the entire world.

The day Jesus was born into this world the cross was always before Him. The cross wasn't some random event God never saw coming. The "Way of the Cross" was planned before the He ever created this world. The Cross is God's statement of love. The Cross is God's love letter to us. There is no greater proclamation of love. There is no other who would give up their Only Son so you could have eternal life. That is the declaration of John 3:16.

I have one son. His name is Landry Jones. I will not sacrifice his life for any of my friends much less any of my enemies. My daughter, Nikki, and my son-in-law, Adam have two sons, Asher and Lucas. I know beyond any shadow of a doubt they would not offer up either one of their sons so that you might live. Landry and his wife, Whitney, also have a son, Ezekiel. Ask them, go ahead I dare you, would they give up little Ezekiel, so you could have eternal life? Oh, don't bother, I already know the answer to that question. No! But, that is exactly what the Lord God did. Without the shed blood of Jesus Christ, we would all be separated from the love of God. Without the shed blood of the Son of God, upon our death we all would be eternally separated from the One who created us. There would be no way to cross that great chasm without the cross.

The Cross, and the death of our Savior is God's love letter to us, written down in the annals of time. That is His declaration and proof of "For God so loved the world that He gave His One and Only Son..." The cross and death of Jesus is our love letter, but the empty tomb and the Living Savior is our Victor's Song!

Today, Kevin and I light the purple "Candle of Love," but remember the red blood of Jesus that was shed for us. This is all the proof we need that God loves us and is for us! Hebrews 9:22 says, "In fact, the law requires that nearly everything be cleansed with blood, and without the shedding of blood there is no forgiveness." Without the shed blood of Jesus, God's One and Only Son, none of us would receive God's forgiveness, and without God's forgiveness we will die in our vileness and be doomed to a place of "great weeping and gnashing of teeth." I invite you today to accept God's great love letter written out on a hill far away and painted red with the blood of His Son.

Questions to ponder and store in your heart:

Has there been a moment on the timeline of your life when you have prayed and believed in the One and Only Son of the Lord God?

If there hasn't been that moment would you like to pray that prayer now and confess "Jesus as Lord?"

If you have had that moment, do you now go through times and you question the Love of Your Heavenly Father?

What can you do to squelch those moments of doubt?

"Lord, I proclaim, "You are love. You loved me so much that You sent Your one and only Son into this world. Lord, I believe in Jesus."

The Dilemma

Day Twenty Three

Have you ever had that problem where life's circumstances weigh on you? You know you need to deal with it, but you don't know where to start. You are facing a dilemma. It is nagging you, and gnawing on your every thought. You go to bed and you are thinking about it. You wake up and there is just something that is pulling on you and you remember, "Oh, my dilemma." It didn't go away with the night. The situation you are facing is on your mind 24/7. It troubles your heart. It perplexes your thoughts. It distresses your emotions. This heaviness and burden won't go away.

That is where we find Joseph today. He had a big problem. He loved this young woman. I call her a young girl. Historians estimate her age to be around 12-14, and she had found herself in the family way. Joseph knew it couldn't be his. A man would know this. She claimed the Holy Spirit of God had overshadowed her and the babe growing inside of her was the Son of God. By law, he had the right to take her to the town square, put her on trial, and have her declared an adulteress. This was a gigantic dilemma for Joseph. He still loved her, but he was confused. He didn't know if she was unfaithful, or maybe she was just crazy. However, what if she is telling the truth? What to do?

Have you been there? You are facing an issue that you see no good answer to. No options appear to be right.

Matthew 1:18-25 records Joseph's story for us. Look at verse 39:

"Joseph, her fiancé was a good man and did not want to disgrace her publicly, so he decided to break the engagement quietly."

Joseph had a plan; not a good plan, and definitely not the plan he wanted. But, it was the only plan he could think of that would allow Mary to keep her life and not be publicly disgraced. It was all Joseph could come up with, but it was not all God could come up with. He had a different plan. God had the "best plan." God had a plan that had been in place since before the days of Creation, and the plans of the Lord cannot be changed. He had already weighed all the costs. He knew the price would be His One and Only Son. He would have to allow a human couple, a couple whom He created, to raise and be parents to His One and Only. God knew the way of the cross all along, but He also knew the Glory beyond the cross. Therefore, God interjected a "but wait" into Joseph's plans.

"This is how Jesus the Messiah was born. His mother, Mary was engaged to be married to Joseph. But before the marriage took place, while she was still a virgin, she became pregnant through the power of the Holy Spirit. Joseph, her fiancé, was a good man and did not want to disgrace her publicly, so he decided to break the engagement quietly. As he considered this, an angel of the Lord appeared to him in a dream. "Joseph, son of David," the angel said, " do not be afraid to take Mary as your wife. For the child within her was conceived by the Holy Spirit. And she will have a son, and you are to name him Jesus, for he will save his people from their sins." All this occurred to fulfill the Lord's message through his prophet:

"Look! The virgin will conceive a child! She will give birth to a son, and they will call him Immanuel, which means 'God is with us.'

When Joseph woke up, he did as the angel of the Lord commanded and took Mary as his wife. But he did not have sexual relations with her until her son was born. And Joseph named him Jesus" Matthew 1:18-25.

Is there a dilemma that is looming over you?

Is there something troubling your thoughts and you don't know where to start?

Are you in a quandary what to do?

When you find your self in that place, your best bet is always to start with the Lord; then do what Joseph did. He obeyed.

God's "best plan" was in place from the beginning. God's "best plan" for each of us has been in place from the beginning also. He has a plan for each of our dilemmas we are facing; we just have to do what Joseph did. He allowed God to interrupt his own plans and Joseph obeyed. He did as the angel of the Lord commanded.

Again, I have it figured out why God chose Joseph and Mary. They had the character types the Lord needed to be the parents of Jesus. They were obedient.

Looking back I have made mistakes when facing dilemmas. I have acted on my own instincts. I have learned that my own inclinations, which are not guided by the wisdom of the Holy Spirit, take me down a very dark and dangerous path. It is a path laden with regrets. Haven't you? I made the mistakes because I felt my plan was better than God's plan. However, I have also faced dilemmas and have chosen God's plan. There is peace and completeness that comes flooding in as I follow God's plan.

Our individual walks with the Lord take many paths as we journey on toward our heavenly home. Each path follows times when we choose His plan and times when we choose our own plans. The path you now find yourself on is the result of one of these decisions. If you have chosen God's plan you are reaping the blessings of obedience. If you have chosen your own way, you are probably reaping the consequences of mistakes made. You may be singing, "I did it my way," and you may not be liking this song choice. Do not fret. God has made a way. He has given each of us an on off ramp that leads to His highway. Jesus said, "I am the way and the truth and the life. No one comes to the Father except through me" John 14:6 NIV. Follow Jesus. He will lead you to the right path. God's grace will reroute you.

Questions to ponder and store in your heart:

What is the dilemma in your life right now?

Is it weighing on you?

Is it on your mind 24/7?

Is there anything that Joseph did that you could apply to your situation right now?

"Lord, life is not easy. Life is filled with dilemmas. God I need Your plans and wisdom. Keep me from messing things up by taking matters into my own hands."

My Christmas Journey

We close out the Advent Season and approach the days of Christmas as Mary and Joseph approach Bethlehem, the village of our Lord's birth. My thoughts have taken me on a journey of my own as I reflect on that first Christmas. The following articles are the compilation of those meditations. I hope you enjoy as I retell their story according to the imaginings of my thoughts. They are The Christmas narrative from my point of view.

Merry Christmas Everyone
From My Heart to Yours

The Christmas Journey

Day Twenty Four

"In those days Caesar Augustus issued a decree that a census should be taken of the entire Roman world. (This was the first census that took place while Quirinius was governor of Syria.) And everyone went to their own town to register. So Joseph also went up from the town of Nazareth in Galilee to Judea, to Bethlehem the town of David, because he belonged to the house and line of David. He went there to register with Mary, who was pledged to be married to him and was expecting a child. While they were there, the time came for the baby to be born, and she gave birth to her firstborn, a son. She wrapped him in cloths and placed him in a manger, because there was no guest room available for them"Luke 2:1-7 NIV.

"But you, Bethlehem Ephrathah, though you are small among the clans of Judah, out of you will come for me one who will be ruler over Israel, whose origins are from of old, from ancient times" Micah 5:2 NIV.

"Now David was the son of an Ephrathite named Jesse, who was from Bethlehem in Judah. Jesse had eight sons, and in Saul's time he was very old" 1 Samuel 17:12 NIV.

Samuel traveled to Bethlehem. He was on a mission from God. Saul had failed again. King Saul didn't have the heart of one who would follow after God, so God chose another. The closer Samuel got to Bethlehem, the more he prayed asking for guidance. As he drew near to the shepherd's home, he became silent for he was listening as God guided him. Samuel wanted to get this right. Saul had broken his heart, and what was worse, Saul's selfish behavior had also broken the Lord God's heart.

Samuel held the chalice of oil. He had come on orders of the Commander of the Angel Army, the Lord God. He had traveled to Bethlehem to anoint the next king of Israel. God had led him to the home of Jesse the shepherd who had eight sons. One by one Jesse's sons paraded before Samuel, and, as each one passed, Samuel heard the voice of the Lord, "This is not the one." "Do you have another son?" Samuel asked Jesse as the seventh son passed before him. "Yes," Jesse replied. "My youngest, but he is a small, ruddy kid still in his youth. He couldn't possibly be who God would choose." "Call him," was Samuel's only reply. As the scrawny young boy approached, Samuel knew, for Samuel had been given the vision to see things as God sees them. "But the Lord said to Samuel, "Do not consider his appearance or his height, for I have rejected him. The Lord does not look at the things people look at. People look at the outward appearance, but the Lord looks at the heart" 1 Samuel 16:7 NIV.

David passed before Samuel. Samuel heard God speak, "Anoint this child."

Hundreds of years later, Micah sat at his writing desk, listening to the words the Lord God was giving him to share with His people, Israel. He was God's chosen prophet at this time. He was the one God was using to turn wayward Israel back to The One True God. God spoke, Micah listened, and he recorded God's spoken message. "But you Bethlehem Ephrathah..."

Hundred of years later, Caesar Augustus was parading through his palace. He was admiring himself and all he had accomplished during his reign. Throughout most of his empire, he was known as the emperor who had brought peace throughout his realm. He thought of himself as the king of peace. He chose to ignore the discontent among his people, and chose to squash any rebellion that might rise up. He carried on with this peaceful facade. Now, he felt an urgency rising up in him. He couldn't place where on earth this urge came from, but he knew he must enact a census throughout his realm. He needed to know how many people he ruled over. He needed a record to be able to receive the proper amount of taxes owed to him.

Therefore, Caesar Augustus issued a decree...

"But when the set time had fully come, God sent his Son, born of a woman, born under the law" Galatians 4:4.

Lord God sat in His throne room. All things were set. He had sent Gabriel to deliver the messages. He used Caesar Augustus to issue the decree. "Out of Bethlehem..." God always knew Bethlehem would be the town where His Only Begotten would enter their world. Satan believes the earth is his domain, but "The Plan" would liberate the captives for all of time. His Angel Armies were surrounding the pregnant woman and her husband. Their swords were drawn and at the ready. Lucifer would not take this plan of attack lying down. God readied His Army for the fiercest attack thus far in this battle between Good and Evil. The Plan of Salvation was His victory march. "The Plan" had been laid out since before the foundation of the world. Lucifer couldn't believe The Creator would be so bold. He couldn't believe that God would stoop so low for those He had created. Yes, God knew Satan would throw the vilest of weapons to thwart this Battle Plan.

"A great sign appeared in heaven: a woman clothed with the sun, with the moon under her feet and a crown of twelve stars on her head. She was pregnant and cried out in pain as she was about to give birth. Then another sign appeared in heaven: an enormous red dragon with seven heads and ten horns and seven crowns on its heads. Its tail swept a third of the stars out of the sky and flung them to the earth. The dragon stood in front of the woman who was about to give birth, so that it might devour her child the moment he was born. She gave birth to a son, a male child, who "will rule all the nations with an iron scepter." And her child was snatched up to God and to his throne.

The woman fled into the wilderness to a place prepared for her by God, where she might be taken care of for 1,260 days. Then war broke out in heaven. Michael and his angels fought against the dragon, and the dragon and his angels fought back. But he was not strong enough, and they lost their place in heaven. The great dragon was hurled down—that ancient serpent called the devil, or Satan, who leads the whole world astray. He was hurled to the earth, and his angels with him.

Then I heard a loud voice in heaven say: "Now have come the salvation and the power and the kingdom of our God, and the authority of his Messiah. For the accuser of our brothers and sisters, who accuses them before our God day and night, has been hurled down. They triumphed over him by the blood of the Lamb and by the word of their testimony; they did not love their lives so much as to shrink from death. Therefore, rejoice, your heavens and you who dwell in them! But woe to the earth and the sea, because the devil has gone down to you! He is filled with fury, because he knows that his time is short."

When the dragon saw that he had been hurled to the earth, he pursued the woman who had given birth to the male child. The woman was given the two wings of a great eagle, so that she might fly to the place prepared for her in the wilderness, where she would be taken care of for a time, times and half a time, out of the serpent's reach. Then from his mouth the serpent spewed water like a river, to overtake the woman and sweep her away with the torrent. But the earth helped the woman by opening its mouth and swallowing the river that the dragon had spewed out of his mouth. Then the dragon was enraged at the woman and went off to wage war against the rest of her offspring—those who keep God's commands and hold fast their testimony about Jesus" Revelation 12:1-17 NIV.

Mary waddled through their home gathering last minute supplies for the long journey ahead. She looked at Joseph with great love and admiration. He was a good man. He was an honorable man. He had prepared a good home, a safe home, for her and this baby she carried. He had come for her even though she carried a child not his own. One day after he had found out about the pregnancy, Joseph had shown up on her father's doorstep. He had come to carry her away to "their home." She always knew, somehow, God would make all things work for her good and for His Glory the moment she told the angel Gabriel, "Let it be done to me as you have said." She knew she had placed her whole life into the Lord's protective care, and now God had provided for her more than she could ever ask, think or imagine. This loving, caring man had provided her and the baby this wonderful home. Joseph had not touched her, not even once. He slept in one room while she slept peacefully in their marriage bed alone. He honored her, and he honored the baby. He would call him son while in public, but in the privacy of their home, Joseph would call Him "Lord."

"Mary," Joseph called her back from her musing. "It is time. The caravan is ready to depart. We must go register in Bethlehem." Joseph saw her gather the rest of her bag. His heart sunk. This would be a hard journey. Her belly was bulging. The Child within her took up her whole midsection. "God!" he cried out. Surely the Lord God would not let His Only Son be born into this world on this arduous journey? "God, I am not that strong. I am not the person You think I am. How can I protect the mother of God on this road?" Joseph silently prayed. The unseen Angel Army walked Mary to the caravan. Swords were drawn as Joseph helped her onto the donkey.

Days later, after many cliffs and dangers had passed, the lights of Bethlehem were in their sights. Joseph was shocked at the crowds. Pilgrims from all parts of the realm were scurrying to their birthplaces. Bethlehem was no different. Hundreds of thousands were pressing into this tiny village. Again Joseph's heart sank. He knew even before he knocked that there would be no room for him in this inn. He had knocked on every door hoping and praying for a small space where he and especially Mary could get some rest. The road had been long and hard. He knew she was uncomfortable on the donkey.

At one point the pain had become so bad he feared for Mary and the Baby's life. He had cried out to God for protection and safety. The pain subsided instantly. He felt a Presence surrounding them. There were no words to describe the safety and peace he felt in that moment. It was like a force from inside Mary's womb had spoken and darkness had fled. This whole journey had been like a life in another dimension.

The course his life had taken was a fantasy. But now, he couldn't accept this. He couldn't possibly believe the Lord God Almighty would allow this. No way would Jesus enter the world in this pandemonium. Surely all of Judah and all of Israel would be made aware that their long awaited Messiah was about to make his entrance. "Not here, God. Not here of all places. Surely not, Lord God. No one is paying attention. Everyone is too busy. People are pouring into this tiny city and no one is noticing this woman who is obviously about to give birth. Is there no one who wants to offer compassion? The only thing the innkeepers are after is the profit they will reap during this census."

Joseph prayed as he knocked at the door of the bustling inn. He knew before the door ever opened what the answer would be. He brought Mary into the light hoping the innkeeper would see her state and be sympathetic to their plight. "There is no room," the innkeeper stated, "but I have a stable out back. Maybe you could make her comfortable in the soft hay." The pains of childbirth were now upon her. The innkeeper's lantern lit the dark path as he led them behind his inn.

The Commander of the Angel Armies had his troops line the darkened way with swords drawn as Mary and Joseph followed the innkeeper. All they could see was the lantern light, but the Glory of the Lord was glowing inside her womb as He was about to make his entrance. "This Light from on High" was about to dawn upon this bustling darkened village. "The Plan" was about to be unveiled, but many would miss it. This was not what they expected their "Deliverer" to look like. However, it would also catch the enemy off guard. The evil leader and his vicious horde would never think of looking in a lowly manger. This manger, this setting, was "Just the Right

Place" for the Prince of Peace to make his royal entrance. It was the place prepared for Mary and Jesus before the foundation of the world. His Angel Army stood with swords and shields drawn. They were a force to be reckoned with. They were His bodyguards.

Joseph could not see the Angel Army, but in perfect peace and complete trust, he raked, cleaned, and fluffed the hay as best as he could. Mary doubled over and fell into the mound with that last contraction.

These words were not recorded for us in scripture. This story was written across my heart as my thoughts mused about that journey Mary and Joseph took so long ago. So many questions tumbled though my mind as I read the account of that first Christmas journey from Nazareth to Bethlehem. God orchestrated this whole sequence. God protected and watched over His Most Beloved Son. Jesus once said as he was being arrested, "Did you not know I could have called down a legion of Angels to help me?" I have to believe a legion of Angels guarded His entrance into our world.

Questions to ponder and store in your heart:

The Psalmist once wrote, "Your eyes saw my unformed body; all the days ordained for me were written in your book before one of them came to be." Psalm 139:16. Can you feel and trust God is watching over you?

God has a plan for your life. What do you think it is?

He who began a good work in you will be faithful to complete it to the very end.

What good work is God doing in you?

Can you trust His faithfulness to complete it?

"Lord, before a day ever came to be for me, You had it planned out. God I know You will complete Your good work in my life."

This Silent Night

Day Twenty Five

"And Joseph also went up from the town of Nazareth in Galilee, to Judea, to the city of David, which is called Bethlehem, because he was of the house and family line of David, to be registered along with Mary, who was engaged to him and was pregnant. While they were there, the time came for her to give birth. Then she gave birth to her firstborn Son, and she wrapped Him snugly in cloth and laid Him in a feeding trough — because there was no room for them at the lodging place. In the same region, shepherds were staying out in the fields and keeping watch at night over their flock. Then an angel of the Lord stood before them, and the glory of the Lord shone around them, and they were terrified.

But the angel said to them, "Don't be afraid, for look, I proclaim to you good news of great joy that will be for all the people: Today a Savior, who is Messiah the Lord, was born for you in the city of David. This will be the sign for you: You will find a baby wrapped snugly in cloth and lying in a feeding trough." Suddenly there was a multitude of the heavenly host with the angel, praising God and saying: Glory to God in the highest heaven, and peace on earth to people He favors! When the angels had left them and returned to heaven, the shepherds said to one another, "Let's go straight to Bethlehem and see what has happened, which the Lord has made known to us." They hurried off and found both Mary and Joseph, and the baby who was lying in the feeding trough. After seeing them, they reported the message they were told about this child, and all who heard it were amazed at what the shepherds said to them. But Mary was treasuring up all these things in her heart and meditating on them. The shepherds returned, glorifying and praising God for all they had seen and heard, as they had been told"Luke 2:4-20 HCSB.

As I sit here and write, I am missing my dad. This will be our first Christmas without him. I write this story in honor of my dad. He was my ultimate storyteller. His ability to weave a tale inspires my love for storytelling. Most of the time he couldn't even finish his story because he was laughing so hard, which in turn had his listeners busting a gut laughing with him. I think he was his own best audience. His absence leaves a vacuum in my family's Christmas this year. However, I know where he is, and I know what he is doing. He is sitting listening to the Master Storyteller weave a story about a Hero riding in on a white horse and on His thigh are written the words, "King of Kings and Lord of Lords." Dad is watching the Lord God prepare for Christ's return. I know there are many of us who have empty seats at our Christmas gathering. This year I will save that seat for Immanuel - God with us.

In memory of my dad:

This Silent Night

Joseph sat helplessly as he watched Mary writhe in pains of childbirth. "It shouldn't be this way," he thought to himself as another contraction doubled her over. Her mother should be with her. Family and friends should be waiting to greet the newborn. Mary needs a midwife not my clumsy fingers. She needs boiling water and sterile sheets, not messy, pungent hay covered in cow dung. Joseph looked at the animals in the stable. Not friends and relatives, but barnyard animals waited for the Birth of a king. This scene was absurd to him. God was about to make his entrance into earth by way of a barn. Mary squeezed his hand and brought him back from his reverie. He wiped the sweat of childbirth from her brow, and as he did, he had a vision of this Son sweating drops of blood in a garden not far from here. He shook that vision away for the time had come. The Child was ready to make His entrance. He held Mary up as she pushed one final time. He pulled the Baby into the world as he had seen shepherds pull baby lambs from their mothers. Joseph placed Him in Mary's arms. He whispered, "Your name is Jesus." The One who had watched and cared for Joseph all of his life was now dependent on Joseph to watch and care for Him. Joseph had trouble dealing with this parody that was being played out in his life.

"Joseph," Mary nudged. "I need the strips of swaddling cloth I packed for the trip. The Baby needs them," she whispered as she caressed Jesus' velvety hair. Joseph wished he had a royal blanket to wrap the Prince of Peace in; instead, he watched as Mary bound swaddling cloth around the Child. Again Joseph saw a vision of this Son being wrapped in grave clothes and placed in a rich man's tomb. The Baby cried; Joseph shook off the vision. The stable was quiet, the cattle were lowing; the Baby slept in His mother's arm. Joseph held Mary; Mary held God. Joseph bowed his head and worshipped the One sleeping in the manger. No one noticed. No one knew. No one cared in this busy city that Royalty had just entered their world. It was the darkest of nights. There was no pomp and circumstance that usually accompanied a king's parade into a city. The tiny sleepy village stayed *oblivious to this Royal entrance. Joseph felt the loneliness of the darkness.*

The Father looked at the vacated throne next to His. He felt the vacuum of the emptiness also. He looked down at the clueless village of Bethlehem. "Aggelos," He summoned the messenger angel. "It is time to make "The Announcement," the Father ordered this messenger Angel. "Don't go to those who are too busy to care. Don't go to those who are too self-absorbed to see. Go to those who are humble in heart. Do you see the land of misfits?" God pointed to a lowly set of shepherds keeping watch over their sheep by night. These were no ordinary shepherds and these were no ordinary sheep. These were the sheep of Bethlehem. These were the lambs set apart for use in the temple sacrifices. These shepherds were regarded by most pious citizens as unclean, and unfit for religious lifestyle. They smelt of sweat and the sheep they raised. "Go to them," the Father pointed out. "Make my announcement known to them alone. For they will remember to worship My Son."

Aggelos flew off and hovered in the silent night right at the spot The Master had pointed out. He waited as God revealed His Glory that lit up this dark night; The Glory of the Lord shone all about the shepherd's field. With a deep baritone voice Aggelos spoke, "Fear not; for, behold, I bring you good tidings of great joy, which shall be to all people. For unto you is born this day in the city of David a Savior, which is Christ the Lord. And this shall be a sign unto you; Ye shall find the babe wrapped in swaddling clothes, lying in a manger."

Then God sent out His heavenly choir to finish "The Announcement." A multitude, hundreds upon thousands upon millions strong, filled the skies. Heavenly Angels, sent by God, began to sing and praise His Only Son. "Glory to God in the highest, and on earth peace, good will toward men." The praise was loud. The worship was honoring. The sound filled the skies and made believers out of these simple shepherds. "Come let us now go even unto Bethlehem, and see this thing which is come to pass, which the Lord has made known to us."

When the Angels were called back to heaven, Creator God spoke and a bright star appeared in the Angel's place. God hung it above His Son; then He caused a group of Astrologers from the east to look up and take note of this new star.

Meanwhile, the motley band of brothers didn't take time to bathe and clean up. They went as they were. Smelly and dirty, and they went in search of this Child they had been told about. When they had come upon the stable, they found Mary and Joseph and saw the baby wrapped in swaddling clothes, lying in a manger. This was their own personal sign, for they themselves had taken sacrificial lambs straight from the ewe's body. Before the sacrificial lambs touched the ground, these shepherds would wrap swaddling cloth around the lamb and place them in a manger. At once the shepherds recognized this sacrificial baby. Jesus had been born to be a sacrifice. He was born for the cross. This humble band of misfits bowed and worshiped the Baby born to die for their sins.

Today Kevin and I will light our last candle in the advent wreath. It is a white candle. It is Christ's Candle. Today this candle will burn in honor of my dad. It will burn in honor of Kevin's dad, whom he misses very much. The purity of this white candle will light up the hole in our hearts because of the absence of loved ones on this Christmas Day. We ignite the wick for all who have an empty seat this year at their Christmas table. As we light it, we will remember Jesus still comes into our messy, smelly lives. He still comes to the misfits and the lonely. He still comes to us personally. Jesus still comes into the darkest part of our lives to light the way. Jesus is Immanuel. Jesus is God with us. And Jesus will come again!

Questions to ponder and store in your heart:

What are your thoughts as you think about the Royal Son of God exchanging His robes of majesty for an outfit of swaddling cloth?

What do you think of as you contemplate Jesus' humble beginnings?

Have you ever wondered if the circumstances you are in were part of God's plan?

What have you faced in your life and you thought, "No way. This couldn't have been what God was leading me too?"

"Lord, the first time You came, You came quietly and humbly. The next time You come the sky will roll back and the trumpet will sound and all will bow before You. Even so come Lord Jesus Christ."

A Village Called Regret

Day Twenty Six

"After seeing them, they reported the message they were told about this child, and all who heard it were amazed at what the shepherds said to them" Luke 2:17-18 HCSB.

As I sit and contemplate the shepherd's message, I think about the people of Bethlehem's reaction. Verse 18 says they were amazed. One translation uses the word awestruck. The Greek word here is "thaumazo," which means to be astonished out of one's senses. I thought about the people in Bethlehem as they heard the shepherds' eyewitness testimony of all they had seen and heard. I wonder, did any of them feel remorse or regret that they didn't offer genuine hospitality or compassion to a young woman who was obviously about to give birth? Did any visitor wish they had given up their nice, comfortable bed? I wonder... This is my story of their regret.

A Village Called Regret

Jesse, the Chief Shepherd, led the way through the cobbled streets. Though it was the darkest part of the night, this sleeping village was still crowded. Caesar's census had caused many pilgrims to come to this small city. Jesse, being the head shepherd, took the lead, as he was accustomed. He had carried many a lamb and also an ewe on his shoulders. They were broad shoulders so he pushed his way past the crowds. He was determined to find this

Child they had been told about. He led his band of brothers through these darkened paths. They would search every stable. They would not stop until they saw for themselves all that had been revealed to them by the Angels. Their Liberator had come. The Word had been made flesh, and they were the first to hear of Him.

They were given a sign. They were to look in a feed trough for a baby wrapped in swaddling clothes, so they bypassed every inn in the city. They weren't looking for the comfortable places; they were looking for the absurd: a Baby in a manger. "What an unusual place for the Anointed One to be found," each shepherd thought to himself. The sight they had just witnessed convinced them of the truth they would find at the end of this quest. It is not every night a host of Heavenly Beings lit up your night sky. They had dropped everything they were doing after they had witnessed "The Announcement" they had received. They didn't bother cleaning up, after all, people were accustomed to their odor. Their profession made them separate from polite and religious society. This manifestation that was told to them was too important for them not to make haste. They were on a mission and Jesse led the way. They rushed down the hill into the streets of Bethlehem to find Him. The Angels had told them peace would come to all who bring pleasure to God. Their path was laid out for them. They didn't hesitate. They knew what they must do; they must go find Him whom the angels sang of.

Jesse saw the stable first. Even before they entered, he knew there was something different about this barn. He looked at his band of misfits. Each had a sense of awe in their countenance. There was expectation and anticipation written on each face. Each had the countenance of a stallion being held back by reins. Jesse looked back at the stable. The hair on the back of his neck stood up. His heartbeat was quickening. There was an aura of peace surrounding this shed. He knew with the next step he took he would enter the stable and he would be brought face to face with the King. Each shepherd entered reverently, and as the angels had said, they saw a new born baby wrapped in swaddling clothes and lying in a feed trough. With this sight before them, they were reminded of the lambs they had brought into the world that were to be used as temple sacrifices. At one time or another, they had each wrapped a newborn lamb in strips of cloth and laid it in a manger to keep it spotless and without blemish.

Jesse fell first before this innocent baby, the others followed suit. Jesse looked to the child's mother. No words were spoken for none were needed. Mary nodded slightly as the chief shepherd reached out to hold the tiny hand. His grimy, sweaty hand that had recently stroked the wool of an ewe, now held onto royalty. At that touch, peace immediately flooded into his heart. All things he had worried about before bedding down in the field to keep watch over a bunch of stubborn sheep were forgotten because he was holding onto the hand of the Prince of Peace. Jesse leaned over the trough and looked into this newborn's eyes - what he saw took his breath away. This innocent baby had the wisdom of one who is ageless. A depth of boundless and endless love could already be felt in the look this tiny child gave Jesse. He felt it to the depths of his being. Jesse felt a love that was from another world in this frozen moment of time. A slight cough behind him intruded and unfroze this moment. Jesse stood to allow others a chance to meet and feel The Prince of Peace. He looked at the child's parents. They weren't at all concerned that this dirty dozen, this group of outcasts, had showed up so soon after delivering God. Jesse studied them for a moment. The shepherds were as awestruck as he was. This was a night to remember.

They were the first to witness heaven coming to earth, besides this new mom and dad of course. One by one each shepherd took his turn to gaze upon The Christ Child. Jesse spoke for the group, "We came in search of something spectacular. We couldn't even guess what we would find at the end of this quest, but it was exceedingly, abundantly more than we could ever think or imagine." He told the new parents about the glorious angel announcing this baby's birth. He then told them about how a heavenly choir came and filled up every inch of the sky singing praises to God for sending The King to the earth. Mary listened intently to every word the chief shepherd spoke to her. She knew first hand what it was like to come face to face with a mighty messenger angel sent from God. She had no doubt this sleeping baby was the Son of the Most High. She looked at Joseph, such a calm and peace had settled over him also. She knew the shepherd's confirmation settled his spirit. An Angel had come to him also in a dream, but it was much needed affirmation to have other witnesses who could testify about who Jesus really is. Their affirmation would fulfill Levitical law of having two or more witnesses to confirm a story.

The shepherds said their goodbyes. They had left their sheep and now they must get back to work. They had been changed because they had witnessed This Child. They had been changed for the better because they had reached out and touched The Prince of Peace. They had first-hand knowledge and now they were busting at the seams to tell their story to every one they met.

They came upon Pando, the innkeeper, first. He had come out of his comfortable bed to see what the commotion in his stable was all about. He held his lantern up high; he started to turn away and pretend he didn't see this group of ragtag shepherds approaching. "What were they doing in town?" Pando thought to himself. "They didn't even bother to clean up before entering our quiet community," he snubbed. Before he could avert his eyes and pretend he didn't see them, Jesse ran to him with such enthusiasm he nearly knocked Pando over. "Excuse me," Pando started to scold, but before he could get another word out, Jesse began an excited and animated account of all that had happened to this ragtag band on this dark night. As he talked, the more enthusiastic he became. Each of the other shepherds started filling in the gaps just in case Jesse didn't quite capture the complete wonder of this night.

With each word spoken more and more people came out of their comfortable resting places to see and hear what this notorious group could possibly be going on about. The shepherd's excitement was contagious. They told their tale at each city block. The whole of Bethlehem soon learned how a young pregnant peasant girl, whom they chose to ignore yesterday, had just given birth to their Deliverer. Pando walked off with a stabbing pain in his heart. The pain was called regret. "How could he not have done more for this young woman and her husband? They obviously needed to be shown more compassion. He should have offered them his bed and his room."

Zoar had traveled with this young couple in the caravan. He chose to ignore the obvious discomfort of the young, pregnant, peasant woman. He had rushed ahead of them upon entering Bethlehem hoping he and his family could get

138

a room in one of the inns. His head hung in shame as he listened to the accounting of the shepherd's. Because of his selfishness, he had missed being apart of the Messiah's story. One by one, each visitor, traveler, and citizen remembered seeing this young couple travel through Bethlehem in search of a place to stay. Each person was filled with regret because they didn't offer compassion to a couple in need.

The bible doesn't tell us whether any of the villagers came to see that which the shepherds had told them about. All we know is a group of misfits dropped everything to see all that the angels had proclaimed to them. I have to believe some of the village people went to worship The Christ Child. The excitement of the shepherd's story had to spur them on to go and bend the knee. If they did, what they found lying in the manger was grace and mercy, which overcame every regret. Regret and failure would have been wrapped up and covered by His love.

Hundreds of years before the birth of our Savior another couple entered Bethlehem. It was a mother and her daughter-in-law. Naomi was the mother and Ruth, a Moabite, was her daughter-in-law. Naomi had left Bethlehem years earlier with her husband and two sons. They had left in search of greater fortune and profit. Naomi returned to Bethlehem broke, a widow, and had lost both of her sons. When she returned she told her family and friends to call her "Mara," which means "bitter." She was bitter toward all. She was bitter toward God. She was bitter because she had lost her family, with the exception of her daughter-in-law who once pledged her loyalty to her mother-in-law saying, "Where you go I will go. Where you lay I will lay. Your people will be my people and your God will be my God." In the end, in this same town of Bethlehem, Naomi discovered a kinsmen redeemer and her daughter-in-law became an ancestor of Jesus our Messiah. In Bethlehem Naomi also found grace and mercy. Grace and mercy took away her regret and bitterness.

I have entered the village called Regret a time or two in my life. Grace and mercy met me as my heart was pierced with the pain of remorse. Grace and mercy healed me and mended all my brokenness. I walked away from that village calling it "Bethlehem," or in Hebrew, House of Bread, because the Bread of Life came and filled me up, and replaced all my regret and bitterness.

Questions to ponder and store in your heart:

My mother-in-law once told me, "I don't want to live with regrets." What kind of regrets or remorse is looming in your heart?

Is there some bitterness in your life that keeps you from moving forward?

I invite you to come and kneel before the Prince of Peace. Come sit with the Bread of Life and let His mercy and grace replace regret and bitterness. Have you met Jesus at the Mercy Seat?

"Lord, thank you for taking away all regrets in my life and covering them with grace and mercy. Help me to forget what is behind and walk forward in newness of life."

After Christmas Special

"After seeing him, the shepherds told everyone what had happened and what the Angel had said to them about this child. All who heard the shepherds' story were astonished, but Mary kept all these things in her heart and thought about them often. The shepherds went back to their flocks, glorifying and praising God for all they had heard and seen. It was just as the Angel had told them" Luke 2:17-20 NLT.

Hi Ho! Hi Ho!
It's Back to Work We Go

Day Twenty Seven

"When the angels had left them and returned to heaven, the shepherds said to one another, "Let's go straight to Bethlehem and see what has happened, which the Lord has made known to us." They hurried off and found both Mary and Joseph, and the baby who was lying in the feeding trough. After seeing them, they reported the message they were told about this child, and all who heard it were amazed at what the shepherds said to them. But Mary was treasuring up all these things in her heart and meditating on them. The shepherds returned, glorifying and praising God for all they had seen and heard, just as they had been told" Luke 2:15-20 HCSB.

It is now after Christmas. I don't know about you, but I hate seeing the last present of Christmas being opened. I really don't like the look of a Christmas tree without any presents under it. I feel like gloomy Eeyore from Winnie the Pooh. Christmas decorations must be taken down, "Oh dear!" I want to rebel. I don't want to get back to normalcy. I still want to celebrate. I don't have a playlist for taking down and storing my decorations. Wonder if I should play Christmas Carols backwards?

Everyone is starting to trickle back to work or at least gearing up for all the new projects that will begin in earnest next week. Accountants will get back to accounting and preparing for tax season. Businesses are buttoning up deals and paying bills to close out the physical year. Hi Ho! Hi Ho! It's back to work we go.

It seems like the world stands still for one day of the year. Peace on Earth lasts 24 hours, and then it is back to our active lifestyle. Have you ever heard about the story of the World War 1 Christmas Truce of 1914? There was a Christmas ad that alluded to it. Time magazine wrote an article about this Christmas miracle. The article explains that over a hundred years ago thousands of British, Belgian and French soldiers put down their rifles, stepped out of their trenches and spent Christmas mingling with their German enemies along the Western front. Some claim this act of peace began with carol singing from the trenches on Christmas Eve. It was a rare moment of peace just a few months into a war that would eventually claim over 15 million lives.

The next day, December 26, 1914, the war resumed in earnest. Mustard gas, real bullets, and artillery shells would claim millions of lives. Many who one day dropped their guns and sang with enemies, were also killed by those same enemies.

And life goes on. Loved ones get sick. Family members are absent, snowstorms hit, and highways get closed. Lives are lost.

I am depressing you, aren't I? I am depressing myself. But you know what? I'm not going to let Christmas end! Christmas did not end the moment after Jesus entered our world as a baby. The party just began. The new mom and dad, and the Baby began receiving visitors. The worshipers came calling!

The angels had carried out their mission. They have gone back to heaven. They are now in an unseen realm. Heaven had touched earth and a group of misfits got inspired. They didn't talk about what they should do. They didn't contemplate what they should do. They didn't go to their new iPhone or iWatch and put it on their calendar. With haste they went to Bethlehem to see this thing the angels had told them about. The Lord had revealed to these shepherds the greatest gift ever given and they went immediately to receive it. They searched every feed trough they were told about. I have to believe there were many animal feed troughs in the village at that time. Bethlehem was the City of David, and according to the Word of God, David would have had many descendants who would have had to go to register in Bethlehem. David had many wives and many children. Bethlehem was busting at the seams during this census. Through desperate searching they found Mary and Joseph and the Baby lying in a manger. They knew the scene when they saw it. These shepherds didn't stop their mission until they worshipped, but after they worshipped, they went back to work. This time their work was different, or at least how they worked was different.

"The shepherds returned, glorifying and praising God for all the things they had heard and see, just as it had been told them" Luke 2:20 NIV. They had been changed for the better because they had seen "The Child." They saw the Son of God who had become a human. The Word had become flesh and they saw it first hand. From then on, I wonder, the next time they wrapped a sacrificial lamb for temple sacrifice, did they think of Him?

Hi Ho! Hi Ho! it is off to work we go. Life goes on after all the tinsel and lights of Christmas, but that first Christmas can change our ordinary workday. Jesus became flesh and blood.

He came to identify with our life. He came so we can celebrate and glorify and praise God throughout the year.

Some, like me, may get the "after Christmas blues." My cure for the after-Christmas Blues is to glorify and worship the King every day of the year. Search Him out just as the shepherds did. They didn't let busy, active people get in their way. They were on a mission to find the Son of God who had become flesh, and they didn't stop till they found him. That is how Christmas can go on and on throughout our whole year!

Questions to ponder and store in your heart:

What keeps you from seeking Jesus?

What did the shepherds do when they heard the news?

What can you do to keep "Joy to the World" echoing in your heart the whole year through?

"Lord, plant the joy of Christmas in my heart Let it sustain me, motivate me, and move me to glorify You my whole year long."

Mary Did You Know?

Day Twenty Eight

"But Mary was treasuring up all these things in her heart and meditating on them" Luke 2:19 HCSB.

I say this every year, "I cannot believe another year has come and gone." Is it me, or does time seem to fly by? We start a new year then we turn around and the year has past. I know we all do this at the close of each year; we reflect and look back at what we accomplished the preceding twelve months. We take an inventory of our lives so far, and we look ahead to prepare for what lies ahead for the coming year. Is our inventory fully stocked? Today I reflect on the lives of all those people who participated in that first Christmas so long ago.

Of all the verses I read, Luke 2:19 still resonates in my heart. I had to look up the word "meditate." Some versions use the word "ponder." The Greek word for ponder is "enthumeomai." We get our word "enthusiasm" from this Greek word. It literally means, "in a state or condition that intensifies a passionate response" or "in a passionate frame of mind." It refers to a passionate supposing or a surmising in a person's mind and heart producing fervent, inner cogitation. Webster's dictionary gives these synonyms - ponder, meditate, muse, ruminate, to consider or examine attentively or deliberately. It implies a careful weighing of a problem.

Mary passionately stored everything that had happened to her in her heart. It was like each event was branded in her heart and mind.

The Gospel of Luke was written by a physician named Luke. Dr. Luke wrote and recorded these events some thirty years after the death and burial of Jesus. He was a believer and he was enthralled with the story of His Savior. He wanted to write to glorify Jesus the Son of God and the Son of Man. I, for one, am so glad he did. He set out to research and interview any and all eyewitnesses of Jesus' life. I have to assume the first place he started was the mother of our Lord, Mary. That is where I would start if I wanted to record accurate events. How I wish I could have been a fly on the wall as Dr. Luke interviewed her. I wonder did Luke feel her passion as she recounted Gabriel's visit? Could he see the tears form in her eyes as she told of Jesus' birth?

She obviously spilled forth every detail of those moments. They are recorded for us in Luke 1 and 2. The Amplified Version of Luke 2:19 says, "But Mary was keeping within herself all these things (sayings), weighing and pondering them in her heart." The NIV says, "she treasured" all these things. The Greek word for treasured is "suntereo." It means, "to preserve and keep safe." The prefix "syn" means "closely together" and the suffix "tereo" is translated, "to guard and keep." Together, these properly mean "to preserve close together with great care and to keep intact." We do not need to question if all of these events are true. They are! They were recorded for us from Mary's eyewitness testimony. When we read, "she treasured these things," literally, she recorded these events, guarded each adventure, and locked them in her heart until the time came for her to tell of her story. Mary would have recounted for Dr. Luke every detail of this blessed event. She would have spoken with deep passion and enthusiasm. It is what a mother would do. It is what I have done as I have told stories about my own children. Don't even get me started talking about my grandchildren. Have you got a candy bar? We might be here a while as I talk about these boys.

Closing a year is always a time of reflection. The last several months of my dad's life I noticed he would take several trips down memory lane. My husband and I made a point of recording some of Dad's stories. I am glad we did. It was my way of preserving the escapades of a great storyteller. That is what Mary did. She preserved Jesus' story. As I close out this year and get ready for a fresh start in the coming year, I want to become like Mary. I want to store and closely guard the gospel, the Good News, of Jesus the Christ. Then, I want to retell His story with the enthusiasm that poured from Mary as she recited for the good doctor the birth of her son, the birth of the Son of God.

"Many have undertaken to compile a narrative about the events that have been fulfilled among us, just as the original eyewitnesses and servants of the word handed them down to us. It also seemed good to me, since I have carefully investigated everything from the very first, to write to you in an orderly sequence, most honorable Theophilus, so that you may know the certainty of the things about which you have been instructed" Luke 1:1-4 HCSB.

The band, "Pentatonix," recently released a new version of the song "Mary did you know?" I listened to it today. I closed my eyes picturing myself in Dr. Luke's place. I pictured myself interviewing the mother of our Savior. I encourage you to listen to the song. As Dr Luke once did, I invite you to picture yourself interviewing the mother of our Lord. Ask her, "Mary did you know?"

Really can you imagine that? You wrap this Child in swaddling clothes and all the while knowing this Child created you. This Child has walked on streets of gold. This Child was there when the earth was formed. All things were created for Him, by Him and through Him. This Child whom she laid in a feeding trough had just come from the very throne room of God!

Questions to ponder and store in your heart:

What all do you think Mary enthusiastically stored in her heart about Jesus?

What do you think about as you reflect over your past year?

What are you doing to treasure Jesus in your heart?

Are you enthusiastic about Jesus?

"Lord, I want to hold Jesus in my heart. I want to treasure and safely guard His gospel, and I want to speak of Jesus with enthusiasm so that those who hear will listen and want what I have!"

God of New Beginnings

Day Twenty Nine

"On the eighth day, when it was time to circumcise the child, he was named Jesus, the name the angel had given him before he was conceived" Luke 2:21 NIV.

"When Abram was ninety-nine years old, the Lord appeared to him and said, "I am God Almighty; walk before me faithfully and be blameless. Then I will make my covenant between me and you and will greatly increase your numbers." Abram fell facedown, and God said to him, "As for me, this is my covenant with you: You will be the father of many nations. No longer will you be called Abram; your name will be Abraham, for I have made you a father of many nations. I will make you very fruitful; I will make nations of you, and kings will come from you. I will establish my covenant as an everlasting covenant between me and you and your descendants after you for the generations to come, to be your God and the God of your descendants after you. The whole land of Canaan, where you now reside as a foreigner, I will give as an everlasting possession to you and your descendants after you; and I will be their God."

Then God said to Abraham, "As for you, you must keep my covenant, you and your descendants after you for the generations to come. This is my covenant with you and your descendants after you, the covenant you are to keep: Every male among you shall be circumcised. You are to undergo circumcision, and it will be the sign of the covenant between me and you. For the generations to come every male among you who is eight days old must be circumcised, including those born in your household or bought with money from a foreigner—those who are not your offspring. Whether born in your household or bought with your money, they must be circumcised. My covenant in your flesh is to be an everlasting covenant. Any uncircumcised male, who has not been circumcised in the flesh, will be cut off from his people; he has broken my covenant" Genesis 17:1-14 NIV.

"God took him outside and said, "Look up at the sky and count the stars—if indeed you can count them." Then he said to him, "So shall your offspring be." Abram believed the Lord, and he credited it to him as righteousness. He also said to him, "I am the Lord, who brought you out of Ur of the Chaldeans to give you this land to take possession of it." But Abram said, "Sovereign Lord, how can I know that I will gain possession of it?" So the Lord said to him, "Bring me a heifer, a goat and a ram, each three years old, along with a dove and a young pigeon." Abram brought all these to him, cut them in two and arranged the halves opposite each other; the birds, however, he did not cut in half. Then birds of prey came down on the carcasses, but Abram drove them away. As the sun was setting, Abram fell into a deep sleep, and a thick and dreadful darkness came over him.

When the sun had set and darkness had fallen, a smoking firepot with a blazing torch appeared and passed between the pieces. On that day the Lord made a covenant with Abram and said, "To your descendants I give this land, from the Wadi of Egypt to the great river, the Euphrates— the land of the Kenites, Kenizzites, Kadmonites, Hittites, Perizzites,

Rephaites, Amorites, Canaanites, Girgashites and Jebusites"
Genesis 15:5-12, 17-21 NIV.

The Eighth Day

Mary looked upon her son. He was both her son and her Savior. He was her new beginning, and He was now eight days old. Eight was the number of new beginnings. A week in the Baby's life had passed. A new day had dawned for Israel. "Forget the former things; do not dwell on the past. See, I am doing a new thing! Now it springs up; do you not perceive it? I am making a way in the wilderness and streams in the wastelan" Isaiah 43:18-19 NIV. The prophet Isaiah had spoken of this newness hundreds of years before this day had come upon the Baby and His new mommy. Mary washed the tiny infant; she was preparing him for "Brit Malah." This was His day of circumcision. Today, she and Joseph would reveal to all what the Baby's name is. As she kissed the top of His head she whispered, "Jesus, your name is Jesus."

She remembered the instructions of Gabriel. She had memorized every word. Gabriel gave her every command the Lord God had given him. "You will conceive and give birth to a son and you are to call him Jesus" Luke 1:31 NIV. Joseph walked up and took the innocent Child from her arms. He tucked the blanket tighter around the sleeping Baby. "Jesus," Joseph also whispered. He could never forget the "dream." An angel had also come to him one night. The angel told him in a dream, "She will give birth to a son, and you are to give him the name Jesus, because he will save his people from their sins" Matthew 1:21 NIV. Joseph held the Baby close and protectively. To the outside world, this Baby was his son, but as he snuggled the Baby closer, Joseph knew this Baby was his Deliverer. "Come, Mary, we should get to the ceremony." With Joseph carrying the Infant, this family of three went to a kinsman's home for the ceremony of "Brit Mahal."

Joseph knocked on the door of his distant relative while he handed the Baby to Mary. Upon entering, Kvatterin took the Baby from Mary and carried him into the room where the circumcision would be performed. All the guests recited, "Blessed is he who comes in the name of the Lord!" Because Joseph and Mary were faithful to the Law of Moses, every ritual of this covenant ceremony was performed to the letter. And now, the Baby held in his body the Mark of the Covenant. Joseph took his Baby back in his arms to comfort and still His quivering chin, and as the wine was poured and the blessing was recited, Joseph put a drop of wine in the Baby's mouth. He revealed to all, "His name is Jesus!" There was a compelling gasp from all the guests. The name meant "God will save." They remembered their mighty hero Joshua. The name held great meaning for everyone gathered. The naming of a child is the most profound spiritual moment in this ceremony. The naming of a baby is a statement of their character. As this Baby slept peacefully in Joseph's arms, every guest there looked upon the One who would save their people.

These are my own thoughts of what probably took place the day Jesus was named. These are customs used in the Jewish ceremony of circumcision. This is the ceremony Joseph and Mary would have followed the day they brought Jesus to be circumcised. According to Mosaic Law, and even before that, God commanded this ceremony be performed on every male child on his eighth day of birth. God made a covenant with Abraham to make Abraham's family fruitful and promised that his descendant's would outnumber the stars of the sky.

In Genesis 17 God performed a covenant ceremony with Abraham. God promised kings and rulers would come from Abraham's lineage. Jesus was a descendant from Abraham. God told Abraham that Abraham's mark for believing in His covenant was the mark of circumcision. Every covenant requires a signature from participating parties. Circumcision was Abraham's mark; it was his symbol that he believed God's promise. On the eighth day of Jesus' life, God also bore the mark of Abraham. The one who made the covenant was now a bearer of the mark of the covenant. On the night that God made this covenant with Abraham, He passed between the carcasses of dead animals in the form of a smoking fire pot with a blazing torch.

If I believe in the trinity, which I do, Father, Son and Holy Ghost and all three are God in One, then I have to see that fire pot with a blazing torch was Jesus Son of God before He came as a baby and entered our world. God the Father, God the Son, and God the Holy Spirit made a covenant with Abraham thousands of years before Jesus received Abraham's mark of the covenant on His body. God the Father, Son and Holy Spirit then changed Abram's name to Abraham. Again, thousands of years before Jesus received his earthly name, He changed the name of Abram and gave him the name Abraham. The paradox and irony and multidimensional parallels in all of this is hard to wrap my brain around.

But for now, as I begin this New Year, my lesson I walk away with is, "God is a Covenant Keeper." He was very specific about when a male child is to be circumcised. A male child is circumcised at eight days of birth. Doctors have discovered at eight days an enzyme is produced in an infant that causes blood to clot faster. Also, the number eight in Jewish religion is the number for new beginnings. Jesus is the only person in all of history that affected our calendar. At his birth the calendar went from A.D. to B.C. We went from counting the days backward to counting the days forward.

Okay, New Year, I am ready to face you. I know my God is a Covenant Keeper! I know my God is a God of New Beginnings! And I know my God will propel me forward and not keep me in the past. I am eagerly awaiting all God has for me, and my family in the coming year!

As my sister blogger, Casey Graves, puts it, "Let's carry Emmanuel - God with us 365 days of the year."

Questions to ponder and store in your heart:

God is the God of new beginnings. What do you want Him to begin in you as you face this new year?

What do you want to restart?

What is His promise to you as you face this New Year?

Whatever promise it is, hold onto it throughout the year!

"Lord, I give You this new year. Lord, it is a restart with You. I hold onto every promise of Yours."

The Presentation

Day Thirty

I am assuming by now everyone has moved on from Christmas, seeing as how we are several days into the new year, and here I am going on and on about the "First Christmas People." Are you asking me if I am still soaring with the Ghost of Christmas past? Maybe you are thinking you should leave this book. Maybe you are saying, "Let's get on with things, shall we?" I should be flying with the Ghost of Christmas Present. So, let's move on to day 40 of Jesus' life here on earth.

"Then it was time for their purification offering, as required by the law of Moses after the birth of a child; so his parents took him to Jerusalem to present him to the Lord. The law of the Lord says, "If a woman's first child is a boy, he must be dedicated to the LORD." So they offered the sacrifice required in the law of the Lord— "either a pair of turtledoves or two young pigeons" Luke 2:22-24 NLT.

"The Lord said to Moses, "Say to the Israelites: 'A woman who becomes pregnant and gives birth to a son will be ceremonially unclean for seven days, just as she is unclean during her monthly period. On the eighth day the boy is to be circumcised. Then the woman must wait thirty-three days to be purified from her bleeding. She must not touch anything sacred or go to the sanctuary until the days of her purification are over. 'When the days of her purification for a son or daughter are over, she is to bring to the priest at the entrance to the tent of meeting a year-old lamb for a burnt offering and a young pigeon or a dove for a sin offering. He shall offer them before the Lord to make atonement for her, and then she will be ceremonially clean from her flow of blood. "These are the regulations for the woman who gives birth to a boy or a girl. But if she cannot afford a lamb, she is to bring two doves or two young pigeons, one for a burnt offering and the other for a sin offering. In this way the priest will make atonement for her, and she will be clean" Leviticus 12:1-4, 6-8 NIV.

I have had a reflective mindset since the beginning of this year. My dad used to say, "I recollect." I guess I have been "recollecting" since January began. I told my daughter yesterday, "My past is what has shaped me into who I am today, but my past doesn't have to enslave me." I have this tendency as I go through January. My family has this saying, "January is going to be a hard month." My dad died January 19th, 2015. My father-in-law died January 23rd, 2014. It is a month that reminds me of sorrow. Dad's birthday was January 26th. I hate writing the word "was." As I was "recollecting," God spoke to my heart, "Your loss is also your dad's gain." My dad believed in the Lord Jesus Christ. He told me his testimony. He spoke it again to me about a month before he died. Really! My loss is my dad's gain. January may at times remind me of death and sorrow, but it also reminds me of celebration. My husband and I celebrate our anniversary on January 5th. My daughter and her husband celebrate their anniversary on January 24th. Isn't that the way of life? Death and sorrow wrapped up in celebration and newness.

Our past definitely shape us. The sorrows it carries pains us still, but the joys of the past enable us to remember God's goodness. We cannot escape all the lessons of the past but we can carry them with us, and if we will let them, the past can propel us into the exceedingly abundant life God has in store for us.

So we cross over. We climb those temple steps as Mary and Joseph did carrying the infant who was both son and Savior. That very first Christmas, the day of Jesus' birth has come and gone, as have the years of B.C. B.C. truly does mean before Christ. There has been no other historical character that has ever changed the calendar. Only one man can claim that distinction. His name is Jesus. It is now day 40 of the year 1 A.D. A.D. is an abbreviation for "Anno Domini," which translates to "the year of Our Lord." We have just begun the years following Jesus birth. The number 40 symbolizes a time of testing and trial. The number 40 relates to a time of humility before God.

The past may shape us but it must not enslave us. The past also has very valuable lessons we must learn so that we can be propelled into Jesus' abundant life He has for us. On this day we read about Mary and Joseph as they were following the Law of Moses written thousands of years before this moment. Mary and Joseph, because they are devout followers of Mosaic Law, follow the law to the letter. God describes Joseph as, "just and upright." He calls Mary, "highly favored." They were faithful servants of the Most High God so of course they would obey Levitical law. On this 40th day of Jesus's life, they wrapped the baby up and traveled from Bethlehem up to Jerusalem to present Him to the Lord at the Temple of God. They would have climbed up the temple steps. This is the first day Mary would have traveled any sort of distance, but it was time to get moving. It was time to get engaged with life again. She had been excluded from church life for long enough. The days of her purification are over now. Get going. Climb up. Put one foot in front of the other and carry your son, the Son of God, up those temple steps. Engage in worship again. Worship the One who sent you this Child. Present your offering of purification. It was the offering of the poor. It was the offering of the peasant people, two turtledoves. Mary couldn't afford a lamb for the morning sacrifice, but on this day she carried that last sacrifice that would ever be needed for the salvation of man. This baby in her arms would be her redemption.

On this day, Mary would have laid her hands on the pigeons. The priest serving at that time would have taken them from her hands and carried them to the southwest corner of the altar, wringing one bird's neck as a sin offering and burning the other as a whole burnt offering. She was now cleansed heart, soul, mind, and body. She could now present her son. The Author of the law was presented before The One who wrote the law in stone, His Father, His Abba. Again, notice the irony of this day. He who had given Israel the purification instruction was now being carried in the arms of one who needed purification. Son of God was now being presented up to God Most High. The paradox of it all is the miracle of this moment. Only Our Loving Heavenly Father would stoop so low so that He could help us climb up our steps into our abundant life. Only He could come up with a plan so unfathomable; and, only He can help us carry our past so that it shapes us into the people He is calling us to be.

Rise up! Climb those temple steps! It is time to engage in worship again! Christ came once to purify us and save us from our sins, He is coming back again to receive us unto Himself; - to restore all that has been lost so that it will become our gain!

Questions to ponder and store in your heart:

Is there anything in your life that is weighing you down and keeping you from God?

Mary had to bring her purification offering. Have you let Christ purify you?

What in your past do you need to let Jesus reshape?

What do you need to cross over and climb up so you can engage in worship again?

"Lord as we face this new year, may we rise up as Your church and climb those temple steps and bring You the sacrifice of worship."

Prompted!

Day Thirty One

"Now there was a man in Jerusalem whose name was Simeon, and this man was righteous and devout [cautiously and carefully observing the divine Law], and looking for the Consolation of Israel; and the Holy Spirit was upon him. And it had been divinely revealed (communicated) to him by the Holy Spirit that he would not see death before he had seen the Lord's Christ (the Messiah, the Anointed One). And prompted by the [Holy] Spirit, he came into the temple [enclosure]; and when the parents brought in the little child Jesus to do for Him what was customary according to the Law, [Simeon] took Him up in his arms and praised and thanked God and said," Luke 2:25-28 AMP.

What was this day like as Simeon woke up and performed his daily disciplines? What did that prompting feel like as he knew he just needed to get to the temple? I think it might have gone something like this:

The Consolation of Israel

Simeon woke up that morning as he had every other morning of his life; he walked to his window and scanned the horizon. For as long as he could remember, he had been waiting and expecting the imminent appearance of the Messiah. This one thing was the platform of his life. He had no doubt; he would never waver; he had centered his whole life around the expectancy of Messiah's appearance. This morning was like every other morning of his life. He opened the window and looked over this city he loved, Jerusalem. The sun was peeking above the hills that surrounded the Capitol. How he loved the view, but how he mourned for his people. They had lost their way. In his heart he longed to see God awaken the Jewish nation. Simeon prayed for God to restore their passion for Him once again. He got to his knees, as he had for many mornings, and he humbled himself in the sight of God. Simeon longed and even panted, as the deer pants for water, to begin his day in the presence of God. Long ago, during one of his walks with the Lord in the cool of the day, the presence and being of God spoke to him. The Holy Spirit of God leaned in close to his ear and whispered a promise to him, "You will not die before you see The Lord's Messiah!" Luke 2:26 NIV.

His name means "obedient listener," and as Simeon, living up to the meaning of his name, heard what the Spirit was saying, and took hold of that promise for all of his days. No matter how long it took, no matter how many years he would wait, this was his life's platform; to wait for the consolation and restoration of Israel. This was his reason for being. This was his life's purpose.

He had received a promise from God and he knew His God would never fail on any of His words. So, every morning, Simeon walked to his window, threw open the shutters and welcomed the new mercies of God. He would look to the rising sun for new rays of sunlight before he would go to his knees to become still and recognize the God who created him. He would listen over and over again for that still small voice he had heard speak the promise to him. This day was no different. To Simeon, God's Word was divine, God's Law was his life; so, he set out to study it as he had done for these *thousands of days of his life. Simeon was a just and virtuous man who cautiously poured over every law and every prophecy that spoke of the coming Messiah. He knew the words of the great prophet Isaiah. He had committed to memory the words of Micah. He knew how the Messiah would come. He knew where the Messiah was to be born. When others were looking for a conquering king, Simeon was looking for the suffering servant.*

Everyday, as he pored over the law and the prophecies, The Holy Spirit of God pressed onto him stronger and stronger and heavier and heavier. On this day, the breath of the Spirit blew across his ears. The hair on the back of his neck rose. He even felt a push on his shoulder. A gentle nudge lifted him from his kneeling position. It was as if he was being led forward. It stirred deep in his gut. This power was propelling Simeon to go. It was an urge. He knew the source. It was the same presence that had whispered the promise to him long ago. In his inner ear he heard, "Go! Go to the temple! Go to the temple and wait and watch!" The whisper floated to his conscious and propelled him forward. Simeon looked to the south of the city toward Bethlehem. A new light was dawning and coming his way. He hurried along. He followed where he was being led as if a person was urgently pulling on his robe, inciting him to make haste. Simeon spoke to himself, he spoke to the air, and he spoke to any who would listen, "The Lord has come!"

Oh to live like that. Simeon lived everyday looking for the Messiah to come. It was nothing Simeon did, but it was everything the Lord did in Simeon's life. It was the Lord who gave him His Promise. It was the Holy Spirit of God that helped Simeon hang onto the promise and it was the Holy Spirit of God that prompted Simeon to get to the temple. All that was required of Simeon was an open heart and a listening ear. Simeon's name means "one who hears and obeys."

Jesus is coming back again. Do I wake up every morning scanning the horizon looking for His imminent return? I do not know the "when" of the word imminent but I do know the "definite" of the word imminent. Jesus has given us prophecies and promises of His return. Am I poring through scripture and learning the signs? Am I committing to memory every promise? Do I wake up every morning comforted by God's new mercies? Oh to live like that!

Let's start scanning the horizon for the return of our Lord. We should each become as burdened as Simeon was over the depravity of our world. We should start preaching the gospel and representing Our King so that all will be ready for the day when the sky will be rolled back and the trumpet will sound to call all believers home!

Questions to ponder and store in your heart:

Describe a time you felt a prompting or a nudge from the Holy Spirit?

Did you obey that voice?

What are you doing to prepare yourself for the Lord's return?

"Oh Lord make me sensitive to Your Spirit. Oh Lord make me sensitive to Your promptings. Oh Lord make me sensitive to Your nudge. In Jesus' name I ask this of You. Amen!"

Holding Onto the Promise!

Day Thirty Two

"That day the Spirit led him to the Temple. So when Mary and Joseph came to present the baby Jesus to the Lord as the law required, Simeon was there. He took the child in his arms and praised God, saying, "Sovereign Lord, now let your servant die in peace, as you have promised. I have seen your salvation, which you have prepared for all people. He is a light to reveal God to the nations, and he is the glory of your people Israel!" Jesus' parents were amazed at what was being said about him. Then Simeon blessed them, and he said to Mary, the baby's mother, "This child is destined to cause many in Israel to fall, but he will be a joy to many others. He has been sent as a sign from God, but many will oppose him. As a result, the deepest thoughts of many hearts will be revealed. And a sword will pierce your very soul" Luke 2:27-35 NLT.

Simeon held onto the promise and he did not let it escape his heart!

I don't know how long it had been since Simeon had received that promise from God, but at some moment on Simeon's timeline the Lord God had told him that he would see the salvation of Israel come to pass in his lifetime.

"The Lord will lay bare his holy arm in the sight of all the nations, and all the ends of the earth will see the salvation of our God" Isaiah 52:10 NIV.

Was it when Simeon had been reading through the prophecies of Isaiah? The Bible doesn't state when God promised Simeon that he would see the salvation of God in the land of the living. God had promised Simeon he would not die until he had seen the redemption of Israel. I do not know how old Simeon was when Joseph and Mary entered the temple courts with the baby Jesus, but when Simeon saw the babe wrapped in swaddling clothes, Simeon recognized the fulfillment of the promise God had made to him once upon a time.

So many questions are raging through my thoughts at this moment. How many promises have I let escape out of my heart because they took too long to transpire? How many promises has God kept in my life and I was too self-absorbed to recognize them? For that matter, how many promises has God made me and I ignored them thinking these were just another verse to read? My heart is aching over my self-centered thoughts and all the promises and fulfilled promises I have let slip away or go unnoticed.

According to Strong's Bible Dictionary a spiritual life is a life animated by the Holy Spirit. It is a life brought to activity by the Holy Spirit of God, and that is how I see Simeon. Every action, every word spoken was moved and controlled by the Holy Spirit who was filling him. Seriously, what person walks up to a young mother and takes her baby out of her arms? That is pretty presumptuous on Simeon's part. The Bible never says that Simeon asks permission. The verse seems to go from point A - in Mary's arms - to point B - into Simeon's arms. Can you even imagine that encounter? Actually, I can. I was sitting by my 5 year old grandson at the Pittsburgh Steeler game a couple of weeks ago, when the guy in front of me began to think of Lucas as a good luck charm. Every time the Steeler's scored he wanted to high-five Lucas. Then, of all things, this guy had the audacity to ask me if he could pick Lucas up. I said. "NO!" So now as I read, "he took the child in his arms" I feel a little anxious.

I don't know Mary's initial reaction. It is not recorded for us in scripture, but I do know both Mary and Joseph's final reaction; - they were shocked out of their senses. Their mouths were agape; not because Jesus was taken from their arms, but because of the words that Simeon spoke over their son, their Savior. No one else knew who this "Baby" was. No one else had been in on the secret. The angel Gabriel had revealed whom this child was, first to Mary followed by Joseph. The Holy Spirit had let Elizabeth and Zachariah in on the true identity of this Baby. The angels had revealed it to shepherds who were watching their flocks at night. Now, to Mary and Joseph's knowledge, that was the extent of the list. No one else knew this child Mary was carrying was the long awaited Messiah. Now this man from seemingly nowhere shows up and recognizes the Christ, Israel's Messiah, the Anointed One, wrapped up in the form of the baby. Come to find out, this man had been waiting all his life for this promise to intersect his timeline.

Simeon, animated by the Holy Spirit of God, spoke words over Jesus that could only have come pouring out because they had been revealed to him by God Most High. Simeon looked past the physical and saw more than a baby. He saw "his promise" come to past. He looked into Jesus' eyes, and, I mean he really looked. He looked deep into those eyes of love and mercy and he saw the light, the true light that would reveal God's true identity to the nations. Simeon saw in Jesus that the glory of Israel had returned. How could Simeon look so deep? How could Simeon see past what looked like an ordinary baby and see his Messiah? Simeon saw and knew because He had been animated by the Holy Spirit of God. God's Holy Spirit, filling Simeon, had helped him cleave to the promise God had made him once upon a time.

Simeon took "The Promise" in his arms and he recognized the fulfillment. Though Jesus was just a baby at this moment when Simeon held him Simeon knew... He knew he was holding his long awaited Messiah. He knew this baby was God's only Son. He knew this baby in his arms had come to reconcile all the world to its Creator. Simeon knew this baby was about to change religion, government, and the hearts of all people.

There is so much I want to say here. So many lessons I get out of the few short verses we get about this man named Simeon, but the one I want to dwell on, the one I want to shout out as a warning to myself and to all others...

Don't let the promises of God escape from your heart no matter how long they take to come to pass! One day you will hold your promise from God in your arms!

Questions to ponder and store in your heart:

What has God promised you?

Has that promise been fulfilled in your life?

From Simeon's example, what can you do to hold onto your promise?

"Lord, help me hold onto every promise written in Your Word. Help me seal up every promise You have revealed to me. Give me a firm grip so that nothing will ever steal Your Promise out of my heart."

You Take That Back!

Day Thirty Three

"Then Simeon blessed them and told His mother Mary: "Indeed, this child is destined to cause the fall and rise of many in Israel and to be a sign that will be opposed — and a sword will pierce your own soul — that the thoughts of many hearts may be revealed" Luke 2:34-35 HCSB.

These had to have been hard words for Simeon to speak out, but I bet they were even harder words for Mary to hear. I am glad I wasn't Mary as Simeon prophesied over my son. I would have yanked my baby back and shouted to Simeon, "You take back those words that you just spoke over my child!"

I studied the sequence of Simeon's spoken words to Mary and Joseph in Luke 2. First Simeon blessed both Joseph and Mary. Do you realize how powerful our words are?

"A gentle tongue (with its healing power) is a tree of life, but willful contrariness in it breaks down the spirit" Proverbs 15:4 AMP.

"Death and life are in the power of the tongue, and they who indulge in it shall eat the fruit of it (for death or life) Proverbs 18:21 AMP.

"For by your words you will be justified and acquitted, and by your words you will be condemned and sentenced" Matthew 12:37 AMP.

I could go on and on with verse after verse about the power of our words. God created the world with just His spoken words, "Let there be...." then there was. We are created in His image so the Lord God put creative power in our words also. With our words we have the ability to speak life or death into a person - inject courage inside a person or fill a person with doubt. I believe this principle with my whole heart. I have lived 54 years and I have seen this played out over and over again, not only in my own life, also in the lives of others I love.

The Holy Spirit of God was now in full control of Simeon as he comes and takes Jesus out of Mary's arms. "The Holy Spirit was upon him" Luke 2:25. Simeon's every action was being animated by God; his tongue and his words are now being controlled by the very Spirit of the Most High God, who is Wisdom Himself. I can't help but notice how Simeon delivers this prophecy over Mary's Son. The sequence of this prophecy is a very important detail we cannot overlook.

First, he blesses both Joseph and Mary. He spoke well of them. He prophesied life into their parenting. With Simeon's words, God spoke prosperity and happiness into Joseph, Mary, and Jesus' life together. Think of it! These two were the parents God chose to bring up and raise His Son. He used Simeon to speak life and wisdom in their parenting skills. I can hear the words, "You can do it! I have given you two everything you need for life and godliness. I will give you the wisdom you will need at the time you need it to help my Son on this journey!" Parents are the first in line to dole out encouragement to their children. Joseph and Mary were the ones God chose to give Jesus a foundation in godliness; so, Simeon blessed them. Words carry power I don't think we fully understand.

The blessing came first, next came words spoken only to Mary. These words would slice through her heart. When Mary heard these words of Simeon's, I wonder did she already feel the knife piercing her soul?

"For the Word that God speaks is alive and full of power (making it active, operative, energizing, and effective); it is sharper than any two-edged sword, penetrating to the dividing line of the breath of life (soul) and (the immortal) spirit, and of joints and marrow (of the deepest parts of our nature), exposing and sifting and analyzing and judging the very thought and purposes of the heart" Hebrews 4:12 AMP.

With Simeon's blessing, Mary's heart was opened. She was softened toward this stranger that had come up and taken her Baby out of her arms. Then came the truth spoken in love. Hard words mixed in with mercy. Piercing words mixed in with the Balm of Gilead.

"This Child is destined, this Child is appointed to be the cause for the fall and also of the rising of many in Israel." This was Jesus's destiny. It was why He was sent to earth. The fall and the rise, the good the bad, the ying and yang - for those who accepted His identity, "the rise" and for those who denied His Lordship, "the fall." That is the paradox of why He came. Simeon saw this as he held his Savior. He looked into the eyes of this mother of Jesus, and with the eyes of God, Simeon saw days and times ahead that the life and death of Jesus would be the sword that would pierce through her soul. Simeon didn't withhold these slicing words; he couldn't. God wanted Mary to hear them. He had to speak what God's Holy Spirit was telling him to say, no matter how hard they might have been to receive. God sprinkled each hard word with softness before them. Jesus, who is the Very Word of God, had come to expose the thoughts and purposes of hearts so that everything could be brought to light and that by His life, death, and resurrection all could be reconciled and restored to God's original intent for man. This is what Simeon saw and knew in that moment of holding "The Promise." He could leave this world in peace because God had fulfilled His Word to Simeon.

Years later, Jesus would try to explain His reason for coming to earth to a group of his closest friends. Simon answered Jesus, "No Lord. May it not be so." Jesus replied to Simon, "Get behind me Satan." At the time Simon spoke, he was not yet filled with the Holy Spirit of God. Only the Holy Spirit of God can help us understand the ways of God. Only the Holy Spirit of God can help us see the power of our words.

Our words can speak life, or they can speak death. It is our choice. Let's be careful what we say to each other!

Questions to ponder and store in your heart?

What have you spoken lately to a friend or a loved one and have regretted saying it?

What can you say to someone that will encourage that person?

Psalm 141:3 says, "Set a guard over my mouth, Lord; keep watch over the door of my lips." How can this verse become a prayer over the words that spill from your mouth?

"Lord God put a centurion guard over my mouth and tongue. Help me speak words of life and edification to my family, my friends, my church. And Lord help me to love and pray for those I don't agree with."

I Can Do That!

Day Thirty Four

"There was a prophetess, Anna, from the family of Phanuel in the tribe of Asher. Anna was very old. She had once been married for seven years. Then her husband died, and she was a widow for eighty-four years. Anna never left the Temple but worshiped God, going without food and praying day and night. Standing there at that time she thanked God and spoke about Jesus to all who were waiting for God to free Jerusalem" Luke 2:36-38.

Anna is our final "Little Women of Christmas." Three verses is all we get to truly glean a picture of our precious Anna, but these three verses is all I need to fall in love with this mighty woman of God. She is my role model.

How did Anna live her life? The first description that is given of our "little miss"...

She was a prophetess. She held an office among the body of those who were looking and waiting for the Messiah. Luke was stating a fact in verse 36. Anna had a gift of communicating and enforcing the Truth of God that He revealed to her. Everyone in the temple knew this about her. Throughout her life, the things she spoke about God, and the things she claimed He revealed to her, all came true. Anna's spoken words were validated from the fruit they produced. Luke had done his investigating. The people who came in contact with Anna knew this about her. Her words were truth.

Next we read that she was Phanuel's daughter. I love that Luke included these five words, "she was the daughter of Phanuel." I am the daughter of James Guy, and I say that with great pride! Anna's dad was a man named Phanuel. The Hebrew word for Phanuel in Hebrew is Penuel. Penuel means "face of God." In Genesis 32, Jacob wrestled with a Mighty Presence who told him, "And He said, 'You shall not be called Jacob any longer, you name shall be Israel for you have struggled with God and with men and have prevailed.'" Genesis 32:38. Jacob then called the place "Penuel" for he said, "I have seen God face to face." So, Anna's dad's name was, when translated, "face of God." Even her own name "Anna," in Hebrew is the name Hannah, which means "grace, favor." She was named after the mother of a mighty man of God - Samuel. In some ways Anna parallels the boy Samuel. Samuel also remained in the temple communing with God. Anna for many years worshiped God night and day fasting and praying. She was the very image of a prayer warrior.

She was from the tribe of Asher. Asher is the last of the tribes mentioned in the "Blessing of Moses" in Deut 33:24-25. This tribe was named after Asher, the son of Jacob. The name Asher means "good Fortune." When Leah, Asher's mother, named him, she said, "Fortunate am I! For women shall count me fortunate!" I love that Anna came from the tribe of Asher. My grandson's name is Asher. Nikki knew it meant "blessing" and our Asher is truly a blessing to us. But all these things were not what gave Anna her spiritual DNA. Her sensitivity to the Holy Spirit of God, her ability to communicate deep spiritual truths from God, came because of her close communion to the living God. Again, like Samuel, she spent every single day of 84 years never having left the temple enclosure. For 30,660 days she worshipped God night and day. Anna practiced the spiritual disciplines of fasting and praying everyday. Obviously she did not go without food for 30,660 days, but at some point during her day, she would put away a time of eating so she could more closely commune with God. What a woman!

A few years ago, I went through a season of panic - especially after each of my children became married. "What am I going to do with myself? What is my purpose in life now that all my energy isn't spent on getting these children raised?" Have you ever had that thought? What is my purpose? Some of the translations say of Anna, "she was aged," or "she was very old." My lesson from Anna... "You can never be too old to serve God." She served God in the temple for 30,660 days by worshipping Him. I can do that! She served God by studying about Him. I can do that! She served God by communicating the truths He revealed to her. I can do that! She served God by fasting and praying. I can do that!

"I can't do everything but I can do something." This is a principle I learned from the Propel Women's Conference. I am not Beth Moore. I am not Christine Caine. I am not Lysa Turkehurst. I am not a nationally known writer and speaker for the kingdom of God. I am Kellye Jones, daughter of James and Peggy Guy, wife of Kevin Jones, mother of Nikki, Magen and Landry, mother-in-law to Adam, Brandon, and Whitney, grandmother of Asher, Lucas, and Ezekiel - that is who I am. My sphere of influence may be small, but it is my domain and my responsibility to be their prayer warrior. I am also a daughter and princess of the King of Kings and Lord of Lords! Until the day the Lord takes me home, I can do what Anna did. I can serve the Lord through worship, prayer and fasting for all whom God puts in my circle of responsibility. I can't do everything but I can do that!

Questions to ponder and store in your heart:

Have you ever questioned your purpose in life?

What can you do that you see Anna doing?

What did Anna spend her days doing?

How could these efforts change our world around us?

"Lord until my dying day may I be found praying and worshiping my God and Creator. May it be said of me as it is written of Anna, "She never left the temple but worshiped night and day, fasting and praying."
Luke 2:37 NIV

Everything We Need

Day Thirty Five

Anna - was she at the right place at the right time, or was it "Divine Appointment" based on "God's Divine Networking?" The Amplified Bible says, "She came up at that same hour." Did Anna just happen to walk up on this holy moment between Simeon, Joseph, Mary and Jesus? I don't believe in coincidences. I believe God takes our lives and has us intersect other lives for His greater purpose and for His glorious plan. This is exactly the scene we read about in Luke 2. However, there is a big X factor here: every player in this scene is highly sensitive to the guidance of the Holy Spirit.

"Coming up to them at that very moment, she gave thanks to God and spoke about the child to all who were looking forward to the redemption of Jerusalem" Luke 2:38 NIV.

Witnessing to others, spreading the gospel of Jesus Christ, is Jesus' last command. It is His Great Commission for all believers.

"Then Jesus came to them and said, '"All authority in heaven and on earth has been given to me. Therefore go and make disciples of all nations, baptizing them in the name of the Father and of the Son and of the Holy Spirit, and teaching them to obey everything I have commanded you. And surely I am with you always, to the very end of the age'" Matthew 28:18-20 NIV.

Scary command, intimidating command, but a commission none the less given by our Commander in Chief, Our Lord Jesus Christ. God has promised that He has given us everything we need to for a life of godliness.

"His divine power has given us everything we need for a godly life through our knowledge of him who called us by his own glory and goodness" 2 Peter 1:3 NIV.

"But in your hearts revere Christ as Lord. Always be prepared to give an answer to everyone who asks you to give the reason for the hope that you have. But do this with gentleness and respect," 1 Peter 3:15 NIV.

God has given us everything we need to obey His Great Commission. I believe our obedience to this commission is in direct correlation to our knowledge of Him who called us by his own glory and goodness. If you will, permit me a moment to reveal the things He is showing me from this glimpse into the scene with Anna, and in the above verses from 1 and 2 Peter.

First off, I see that Anna has placed herself under God's amazing umbrella. She is prayed up, and studied up. She has made herself available to God. Her heart condition is pliable and sensitive to the leading of the Holy Spirit. Where the Holy Spirit leads, she will go in obedience. So much so that when a divine appointment comes along she recognizes it immediately. "At the exact moment Simeon is praying she walks up." I love the sound of God's people praying together. Kevin and I audibly pray together at night. I love the sound of the prayers. I think God loves to hear them also. Kevin agrees with me, "Yes Lord Yes Lord." I agree with him, "Yes and Amen Lord Jesus!" Throughout our prayer time each of us are audibly agreeing with the other and at times the hair on my arms sticks up. God is in our prayer times!

"For where two or three gather in my name, there am I with them" Matthew 18:20 NIV.

This was my verse during my last trip to Ethiopia. We would gather for prayer before starting each day. Our mission team would start our time with singing "Amazing Grace," then each of us, both American and Ethiopian Christians, would begin praying and agreeing with each other in prayer. "Yes Lord, yes Lord, we call on Your Name Lord." My emotions tend to lean toward the weeping side. Tears would be flowing as a result of the sweet sound of the brethren and sisters in Christ calling out to God in unity. At times when you can feel "The Presence of the Lord in this place" in the gardens of the Hilton Hotel of Addis Ababa, Ethiopia. "Coming up to them at that very moment, she gave thanks to God and spoke about the child to all who were looking forward to the redemption of Jerusalem." As I read those words I can hear saints harmonizing in corporate prayer. You can hear Anna proclaiming to all, "Praise to You Lord God for the Redemption of Israel. Salvation has come." or words of worship to that effect. At the same moment Simeon was praying, Anna was praising and spreading the good news about who this baby was. If this sound moves me, I can only imagine how it moves Lord God! The sound of prayer and unity among His children! This is the sound I hear in these verses.

At that moment... Anna was at the right time, in the right place, and among the right people. She was prepared for this divine appointment. That is the lesson I take away from this look at Anna's life. She was prepared in season and out to give an answer for her joy and hope. She had spent her life in communion with God. That is our key to obeying God's Great Commission. Before we go out into the world and proclaim the good news of Jesus Christ, we must first "come into His presence" as Anna had done her whole life. Then, the good news flows out of us.

I agree obeying the great commission is a daunting and intimidating task, but it is a command that God will help us obey and be ready for. The gospel will flow out of us because we have been in the Presence of our King.

The other day Kevin was prepared for a random conversation with his Muslim Uber driver. He had spent time with the Lord that morning studying God's Word and in prayer. He was ready and armed with the Gospel of Jesus Christ. God's Word and time spent with God had emboldened him and infused him with courage. He was ready to tell this man of different faith the reason for his hope in Jesus Christ.

Divine appointments and divine networking happen everyday. We will be able to recognize them as Anna did when we have come into the Presence of God!

Questions to ponder and store in your heart:

How can you be ready to tell people about the hope you have in Jesus Christ?

How can you be sensitive to God's appointments?

How was Anna ready for God's divine appointment?

Have you ever had a moment when you knew God had placed you here? Describe that time.

"Lord make me available in season and out of season to always be ready to give an answer for the hope I have which is in Christ Jesus my Lord. Make me sensitive to Your divine appointments."

What About That Star?

Day Thirty Six

"Jesus was born in Bethlehem in Judea, during the reign of King Herod. About that time some wise men from eastern lands arrived in Jerusalem, asking "Where is the newborn king of the Jews? We saw his star as it rose, and we have come to worship him." King Herod was deeply disturbed when he heard this, as was everyone in Jerusalem. He called a meeting of the leading priests and teachers of religious law and asked, "Where is the Messiah supposed to be born?" "In Bethlehem in Judea," they said, "for this is what the prophet wrote: 'And you, O Bethlehem in the land of Judah, are not least among the ruling cities of Judah, for a ruler will come from you who will be the shepherd for my people Israel.'"

Then Herod called for a private meeting with the wise men, and he learned from them the time when the star first appeared. Then he told them, "Go to Bethlehem and search carefully for the child. And when you find him come back and tell me so that I can go and worship him, too!" After this interview the wise men went their way. And the star they had seen in the east guided them to Bethlehem. It went ahead of them and stopped over the place where the child was. When they saw the star, they were filled with joy! They entered the house and saw the child with his mother, Mary and they bowed down and worshiped him. Then they opened their treasure chests and gave him gifts of gold, frankincense, and myrrh" Matthew 2:1-11 NLT.

The Star

The Creator spoke and it was. The angels looked on, marveling at His mighty works. It seemed El Elyon - The Most High God - had a specific place and purpose for everything He was creating. Now what did He call these shiny twinkling things that filled the night sky? Oh yeah! He called them stars. The Mighty God hung each star in a specific place. "They tell my story," He told the angels who were watching Him create. "See that grouping over there, in the shape of a woman, they speak of a virgin mother." Each Angel could tell He enjoyed creating. He would speak and the Son, who is the very Word of God, would hang each star. The Spirit of God hovered over all that was being created and breathed life into everything. The whole act of creation was awe-inspiring and each angel couldn't turn away. After hanging each of the stars in a specific place the Father handed the Son His distinct star to hold onto for the perfect time in space. "One day Son, we will hang this star together and it will hold a special purpose for those who notice it." The trinity went back to work on the rest of creation.

Elyasar noticed it first. He was the wisest of the wise. He had all the mathematical figures down as he had studied the stars for all of his life. He knew the locations of each. The stars had guided his way during his travels countless times before. Now, the kings of the east had called upon him and his fellow astrologers to help interpret the stars for them so that they could make decisions based on the alignment of the stars. This was the way of their religion. The stars guided their life. As head astrologist, it was Elyasar's duty to scan the night skies, and he was certain his charts were accurate. He noticed this new star immediately. Its twinkling light had never appeared before in all his days. Even the way it shined amongst all the other stars was different, brighter, bolder, and of higher clarity. He pulled out old parchments from among his historical shelves, and specifically searched among the prophets of the Jewish people. He recalled stories that had been handed down through the ages during the time the nation of Israel was exiled among his people and his land. He vaguely remembered the stories they told of a Most High God - how He created all things and hung the stars in specific places to tell a story of redemption. Somehow, Elyasar knew this new heavenly body shining so brightly in the night sky was part of El Elyon's story of salvation. He gathered his belongings and gathered his fellow stargazers, for he was about to start a journey. He was going to follow the star wherever it led him. Elyasar knew in the depths of his being that whomever they found under this unusual star was worth the long arduous journey that lay ahead of him! Somehow, Elyasar knew this star would lead him to a king.

Of course, I am in my story telling mode. I have no idea what the names of the wise men were. The Bible doesn't give them. Their names are not important, but what is important is what they did when they discovered this new star that had risen in the east. They set out on their camels and followed it. They let this star be their guide to help them find the new King.

We also have a guide that leads us to the King of Kings and Lord of Lords - the very Word of God, our Bible. Does yours have dust on it? For a season in my life mine had collected layers and layers of dust. I had replaced my Bible for emails and Facebook. My life seemed to be going nowhere. I had no guidance. My soul was longing for God's direction but I was feeding it social media. I was slowly shriveling. I had lost my way. As I unpacked my new house, I unpacked a couple of boxes of books. I had a front room with a bookcase, and wanted to fill it. I held my old Bible that was so worn out the binding was falling off. It seemed as if it was calling me. Just as Elyasar knew the new star would lead him to a King, I knew this book I held in my hand, with its tattered binding and edges, could guide me back to where I belonged.

"In the beginning God created the heavens and the earth. Now the earth was formless and empty, darkness was over the surface of the deep, and the Spirit of God was hovering over the waters. And God said, "Let there be light," and there was light. God saw that the light was good, and he separated the light from the darkness. God called the light "day," and the darkness he called "night." And there was evening, and there was morning—the first day. And God said, "Let there be a vault between the waters to separate water from water." So God made the vault and separated the water under the vault from the water above it. And it was so. God called the vault "sky." And there was evening, and there was morning—the second day" Genesis 1:1-8 NIV.

"I see him, but not now; I behold him, but not near. A star will come out of Jacob; a scepter will rise out of Israel. He will crush the foreheads of Moab, the skulls of all the people of Sheth" Numbers 24:17 NIV.

"He determines the number of the stars and calls them each by name" Psalm 147:4 NIV.

"When I consider your heavens, the work of your fingers, the moon and the stars, which have set in place," Psalm 8:3 NIV.

Questions to ponder and store in your heart:

Have you ever gone through a time when you felt you were drifting? Describe it

Where do you go when you have questions about life events?

Just start! How long has it been since you have followed your star and read your bible?

How can the bible become your star and guide you to make decisions for your life?

"Lord Your Word is a light unto my feet and a lamp unto my path. God please help me follow Your commands and precepts."

They Looked in All the Wrong Places

Day Thirty Seven

"After Jesus was born in Bethlehem in Judea, during the time of King Herod, Magi from the east came to Jerusalem and asked, "Where is the one who has been born king of the Jews? We saw his star when it rose and have come to worship him." When King Herod heard this he was disturbed, and all Jerusalem with him. When he had called together all the people's chief priests and teachers of the law, he asked them where the Messiah was to be born. "In Bethlehem in Judea," they replied, "for this is what the prophet has written: " 'But you, Bethlehem, in the land of Judah, are by no means least among the rulers of Judah; for out of you will come a ruler who will shepherd my people Israel.' " Then Herod called the Magi secretly and found out from them the exact time the star had appeared. He sent them to Bethlehem and said, "Go and search carefully for the child. As soon as you find him, report to me, so that I too may go and worship him." After they had heard the king, they went on their way, and the star they had seen when it rose went ahead of them until it stopped over the place where the child was. When they saw the star, they were overjoyed. On coming to the house, they saw the child with his mother Mary, and they bowed down and worshiped him. Then they opened their treasures and presented him with gifts of gold, frankincense and myrrh. And having been warned in a dream not to go back to Herod, they returned to their country by another route" Matthew 2:1-12 NIV.

What about this star? Apparently, the star the wise men had been following merely led them to general vicinity - the Judean hillside of Israel. Bethlehem and Jerusalem are located in this area. Bethlehem is six short miles from Jerusalem. The wise men stopped short. They went looking for the King of the Jews in the capital city of Israel - Jerusalem. That makes sense when you think about it. Jerusalem was a thriving metropolis. Bethlehem was a tiny village; home to perhaps 200 permanent residents. Bethlehem was a pit stop on your way to the big city. These wise men weren't so wise at this point. They bypassed the birthplace of a king because they assumed he would be found in the capital city. What seemed to be an obvious place to start was actually not so obvious. They carried with them their own assumptions of where a king ought to be. Bethlehem was so close - just six miles away, but they began their search in the wrong city.

How many ways past Sunday does that assumption speak to me? How many spiritual lessons does their misleading ideas teach me? How many times have I missed an encounter with Jesus because he was working where I believed He wouldn't work? Jesus was alive and active and at work in places I would never think to look! Isn't that how He lived out His days as He taught and ministered during those three years He walked this planet? He ate and banqueted with the sinners and scoundrels. He did not come for the self-righteous Pharisees and Sadducees. He ate with the tax collectors and the despised. He healed the demon possessed and the lepers. He went to those that the religious society had cast out. Jesus was born not in the capital city of Israel but in the tiny village south of Jerusalem.

These wise men were astrologers from the east. They were not of Jewish descent. Their religion was steeped in eastern mysticism and astrology. They made their decisions and advised kings based on the alignment of Virgo, Leo, The Age of Aquarius, and all the others. They worshiped according to the Zodiac signs and not because of the Bright and Morning Star. They knew there was a new star shining above. They knew it meant the King of the Jews had been born, but they were missing some data. They didn't have the Torah to guide them. They only had stories they were told; they did not have the writings of the Law and Prophets. They needed someone to fill in the gaps. Again, how many times have I missed having an encounter with Jesus because I had gaps in my knowledge of who He really was? I had depended on the stories and the faith of others, and chose not to go deeper in my relationship with Him through my own study and knowledge of Him.

These wise men stopped short of finding their King right away because they made a wrong assumption based on their lack of all the data. King Herod and the scribes and Pharisees had all the data; they knew where the King of the Jews would be born. But yet... But yet they did not go. Herod sent the wise men. Really? What's up with that? A King had been born to them. I get Herod. He was jealous, but why didn't these Jewish scholars go? They knew the answer right away. They didn't even have to consult their parchments. They knew the Law and Prophets by heart. They had the words of Isaiah and Micah memorized. When they learned of the star, how come they didn't pack up and go with these astrologers?

There were two differing heart conditions here. Though these wise men had made wrong assumptions and didn't know the Torah, they still had come on this quest so that they could worship this new King. "We saw His star as it rose, and we have come to worship Him." When the scribes and Pharisees heard of the star they were deeply troubled. Uh Oh, someone new was about to upset the apple cart. Someone was going to shake the status quo. They didn't go to worship the King because they were spiritually indifferent and too puffed up with themselves. They were culturally arrogant and lazy. They could have walked six short miles in a day, but they chose not too. Instead, Herod chose instead to send wise men from a different religion to go and check it out.

How many times have I chose not to go on my own spiritual quest, seeking a deeper relationship with Jesus, because I was spiritually indifferent? The instantaneous gratification of watching TV or surfing the internet quelled an immediate need and kept me occupied so I wouldn't go on a time consuming voyage into a deeper relationship with my Savior. Shorter term for all that would be laziness. I have been putting off sitting down at the computer because I knew once I started writing on this subject I would be stepping on my own toes. I have skipped having my morning quiet times over the past couple of days and, boy, have I been irritable.

My spiritual lesson #1,000,001... Six short miles. Don't stop short. The hike is worth it! Quit being lazy. Quit living off of other's faith. Underneath the Star you will find your King.

Questions to ponder and store in your heart:

Where did the wise men look first to find the new King of the Jews?

What wrong assumptions have you made about Jesus?

Have those assumptions caused you to miss what Jesus is doing in your life?

Have you allowed life to cause you to stop short of seeking Jesus and the abundant life He has for you?

"Lord make me bold enough to follow Your star wherever it may lead me."

The Right Stuff

Day Thirty Eight

"Then Herod called for a private meeting with the wise men, and he learned from them the time when the star first appeared. Then he told them, "Go to Bethlehem and search carefully for the child. And when you find him come back and tell me so that I can go and worship him, too!" After this interview the wise men went their way. And the star they had seen in the east guided them to Bethlehem. It went ahead of them and stopped over the place where the child was. When they saw the star, they were filled with joy! They entered the house and saw the child with his mother, Mary, and they bowed down and worshiped him. Then they opened their treasure chests and gave him gifts of gold, frankincense, and myrrh. When it was time to leave, they returned to their own country by another route, for God had warned them in a dream not to return to Herod" Matthew 2:7-12 NLT.

Did you ever see the movie, "The Right Stuff?" It was released in 1983. My oldest was a year old. Great movie no matter how old it is. It was an epic drama about NASA's search for the first astronauts and the early years of America's space program. Seven military pilots were selected to be astronauts for Project Mercury. The pilots went through a series of stringent tests. Each candidate was out to prove they have the "right stuff" to become America's first astronauts.

Why do I bring up that movie? I ask myself those same questions when thoughts like that flow through my brain as I read about people in the Bible. I guess that is what I see in these wise men from the east. They were made of "The Right Stuff." They were adventurous enough to leave their country and travel thousands of miles through unknown territory to follow a new star. Their hearts were open to worshiping a new king. They were humble enough to ask for directions, and they were wise enough to bring the right baby gifts. Though they took a detour and asked for directions, they weren't distracted by the magnificence of the Jewish temple, or the opulence of Herod's palace. They didn't find who they were looking for among all the glitz and the glitter, so they kept looking. They displayed endurance and perseverance. They left the high and mighty king behind, the star shone brightly for them once again. "After this interview the wise men went their way. And the star they had seen in the east guided them to Bethlehem." I wonder, what happened to the star before their stop? Why did it suddenly come back into their view? Maybe it was shining all along, but they were distracted by the glory of the temple, with its white marble facade and golden capitals? Or, maybe, God obscured the star to test the wise men's resolve to follow it no matter where it led? The Bible doesn't say, but there is great spiritual truth to be learned by asking these questions.

Still, I keep thinking these wise men were made of "The Right Stuff." The NIV translation says, "When they saw the star, they were **overjoyed.**" I love seeing that adjective about them. It is not just joy, or joyful, or filled with joy. **Their joy was overflowing and sloshing out!** The thing that had guided them, the one thing that was leading them to the King of the Jews, was back. Their GPS started working again. Do you know that feeling? Boy I do. I hate it when I hear my system say "rerouting" or "off-route" or "unmapped road." Yeah I hear that a lot. I kind of like to "Dora the Explorer" my way around unknown cities, so it does make me joyful to hear "proceed on this highway." As I have mentioned before, I view the star that guided them in the same manner as I view God's Word as it guides me through this pilgrimage. If I will follow it, I will also find my King. My question I am asking myself, "Am I overjoyed to follow my atlas?" Overjoyed. Yeah I would call that a characteristic of having "The Right Stuff."

"They entered the house and saw the child with his mother." This is the King the star had led them to. Jesus didn't have servants bowing to His every whim. He wasn't being taught and trained in the art of war as most princes these men were accustomed to beholding. This new King was with his mother. He wasn't in a setting they were used to witnessing. He was in a home, a house. It was a normal dwelling place. This King did not look like the kings they were accustomed to meeting. This King would not need their advice. This King would not consult the stars for direction. This King would consult the One who created each star and hung it in place. No, this King was not what they expected, but they did not let their expectations damper their worship. "When they saw the child with Mary, they bowed down and worshiped." They worshiped the King in spite of their false expectations. Yeah, I call that "The Right Stuff."

"They opened their treasure chests and gave him gifts of gold, frankincense and myrrh." They came prepared to give gifts befitting a king. Gold, frankincense and myrrh were standard gifts to honor a king or deity in ancient times. They offered tribute money to a King. They regarded Jesus as Royalty. In my mind, they were the first Gentile worshipers of the King of Kings and Lord of Lords. Their religion was pagan, but these pagan dignitaries did more than the scribes and Jewish scholars of that day did. They bowed down to worship. Their gifts were most likely a whole train of pack animals loaded with gold, frankincense, and myrrh. Gold is the gift to honor a king. Frankincense is the incense burned in religious ceremonies, and myrrh is the oil that is used to anoint a dead body before burial. Each of these gifts was symbolic of the ministry of Christ as he walked on earth. They brought "The Right Stuff" to the baby shower. I went to my future grandson's baby shower. I gave him an organic mattress his mommy had picked out for this precious child. I considered it "The Right Stuff." However, it is nothing compared to the honor these wise men paid this King.

These wise men traveled over 1000 miles to come and worship. They were made of "The Right Stuff." They had hearts open to seeking the King of the Jews.

Questions to ponder and store in your heart:

What examples of the "Right Stuff" do you see in these wise men?

What adventure is God calling you to?

When you find the King of Kings and Lord of Lords, what will you do to worship Him?

What gifts are you offering "The King" that are made of the right stuff?

"Lord give me 'The Right Stuff'. Put a seeking, open heart in me. Take out this heart of stone and give me a heart of flesh that seeks You no matter what. Give me an adventurous spirit to follow You wherever You lead."

El-Olam – The God Who Sees Beyond Our Vanishing Point

Day Thirty Nine

"When it was time to leave, they returned to their own country by another route, for God had warned them in a dream not to return to Herod. After the wise men were gone, an angel of the Lord appeared to Joseph in a dream. "Get up! Flee to Egypt with the child and his mother," The angel said. "Stay there until I tell you to return, because Herod is going to search for the child to kill him" That night Joseph left for Egypt with the child and Mary, his mother, and they stayed there until Herod's death. This fulfilled what the Lord had spoken through the prophet: "I called my Son out of Egypt" Matthew 2:12-16.

"Then Abraham plated a tamarisk tree at Beersheba, and there he worshiped the Lord, the Eternal God (In Hebrew - El-Olam)" Genesis 21:33 NLT.

"A great sign appeared in heaven: a woman clothed with the sun, with the moon under her feet and a crown of twelve stars on her head. She was pregnant and cried out in pain as she was about to give birth. Then another sign appeared in heaven: an enormous red dragon with seven heads and ten horns and seven crowns on its heads. Its tail swept a third of the stars out of the sky and flung them to the earth. The dragon stood in front of the woman who was about to give birth, so that it might devour her child the moment he was born. She gave birth to a son, a male child, who "will rule all the nations with an iron scepter." And her child was snatched up to God and to his throne. The woman fled into the wilderness to a place prepared for her by God, where she might be taken care of for 1,260 days." Revelation12:1-6 NIV

"Put your sword back in its place," Jesus said to him, "for all who draw the sword will die by the sword. Do you think I cannot call on my Father, and he will at once put at my disposal more than twelve legions of angels?" Matthew 26:52-53 NIV.

The Eternal God. El-Olam. The name literally meant "to be hidden." It speaks of something that cannot be seen or perceived. The idea is that there comes a point in this world where our senses reach their absolute limit, like when we look at the horizon ahead of us and can't see any further. Some scholars have defined "olam" as the vanishing point. Our Eternal God transcends what we can see and measure with our finite senses. He can see all things that are beyond our vanishing point! Take a moment to look up and see your horizon. Look at the very furthest point that you can see with your vision. Now think about this - God sees what is beyond that last focal point of your eyesight!

Mind Blowing! Boom! There is a sign for awesome. You place your fingertips together at your temples, then pull away and signal them blowing apart. That is the sign for awesome. That is the sign for mind blowing. That is the sign for El-Olam. Eternal God. That is who was warning the wise men in these verses. The Eternal God. That was who warned Joseph. El-Olam. Abraham worshiped El-Olam thousands of years before Joseph was charged with keeping "The Eternal God made flesh" safe. Wrap your head around this thought - before the Father sent His Son into the world, He promised His Son safekeeping. That is why Jesus told Peter, "Put your sword away. Do you think I cannot call on my Father, and He will at once put at my disposal more than twelve legions of angels?" Matthew 26:52-53 NIV.

The Eternal One - the One who sees beyond the vanishing point, knew danger was coming down the mountain. I can see it in my thoughts now; more than 12,000 legions of angels were surrounding Mary, Joseph, and the Child Jesus at that very moment. The Eternal God saw evil hordes coming. "Get up!" "Right now, get up! Flee to Egypt!" The hordes of hell were fast approaching trying to thwart the Plan of Salvation for all mankind. Their instrument of evil was the jealousy of King Herod. El-Olam, The Eternal God, knew this evil would be coming before a single day was created. El-Olam, The Eternal God, warned the wise men, "Don't go back to Herod." The Eternal God saw beyond their vanishing point. Maybe they thought they could read about this evil in the stars that guided them, but the One who created the heavens, led them away from the danger He foresaw coming their way if they went back to Herod.

El-Olam. Our Eternal God. He sees all that is beyond our vanishing point. He provides escape routes and He sends us provisions beforehand for all that we might need. Where did Joseph get the money to help his family escape to safety? His son, the Son of God, was given a whole camel train laden with gold, frankincense, and myrrh. El-Olam. The Eternal God provided for their needs before their need arose because He saw beyond Joseph's vanishing point!

He is still El-Olam. He has not changed. These are turbulent times. Our future is unknown. We can take on all kinds of worry for what is unseen and lying ahead, or, and I say again, or! We can trust El-Olam, our Eternal God who is going to provide for all unknown needs!

Questions to ponder and store in your heart:

What future events are you worried about?

What does it mean to you that God sees beyond our vanishing point?

How can you trust God with your unknown future?

What are your thoughts when you call God your Eternal God?

"Lord, no matter what, You hold my future in Your hands. You see things that are beyond my horizon. I will trust in You."

God Has it All Mapped Out

Day Forty

"After they had gone, an angel of the Lord appeared to Joseph in a dream and said, "Get up, take the child and his mother and flee to Egypt, and stay there until I tell you, for Herod is going to look for the child to kill him." Then he got up, took the child and his mother during the night and went to Egypt. He stayed there until Herod died. In this way what was spoke by the Lord through the prophet was fulfilled: "I called my Son out of Egypt" Matthew 2:13-15 NET.

"When Israel was a child, then I loved him and I called My son out of Egypt" Hosea 11:1 NLT.

"After Herod had died an angel of the Lord appeared in a dream to Joseph in Egypt saying, "Get up, take the child and his mother, and go to the land of Israel, for those who were seeking the child's life are dead." So he got up and took the child and his mother and returned to the land of Israel. But when he heard that Achelaus was reigning over Judea in place of his father Herod, he was afraid to go there. After being warned in a dream, he went to the regions of Galilee. He came to a town called Nazareth and lived there. Then what had been spoken by the prophets was fulfilled, that Jesus would be called a Nazarene" Matthew 2:19-23 NIV.

"So when Joseph and Mary had performed everything according to the law of the Lord, they returned to Galilee, to their own town of Nazareth" Luke 2:39 NET.

I like to "Dora the Explorer" my way around new cities. I know that all roads lead to somewhere. I am pretty good navigationally. The only time I am navigationally challenged is coming out of hotel rooms. Invariably I turn the wrong direction when coming out of my room. My husband is fine with it. He lets me wander off going the wrong way. This is our modus operandi. I go the wrong direction. He waits for me by the door. I turn and see he is not following me but is ready to head the right way toward the elevator. I do not know what happens to me every time we check into a hotel, but it is like my biological GPS switches off. Now, get me outside and north, south, east, and west just come to me, and boy, if you ever let me see a map of the city I am in, it is Katie bar the door. I am spot on at being your navigational guide. I like to see the big picture. I like to see what suburbs lie in the North or what mountain ranges border the west. You catch my drift.

I visit Addis Ababa, Ethiopia quite often. I have never been shown a map of the city; therefore, I have to make landmarks so I can know where I am at all times. I don't drive in Addis. No way! That would be dangerous for me. We have a driver and I have my landmarks. The problem with this is sometimes we circle the same landmark over and over again. I do not know how that happens. I do know, however, that when I pass the muddy area where all the people are washing cars manually, I am about to turn into the Bole district of Addis where the feeding center is. I do know when I pass all the shepherds and their herds I am on the right road to head to the homes of IAMNOT4GOTTEN MINISTRIES. My point being, I like to know that I am on the right road. In a perfect world, I like to see the big picture of the map of my life so that I can know the road I am now on is leading me down the path

God has for me. That is my perfect world. That is what makes me feel safe and secure. That is what keeps anxiety at bay for me.

But guess what? Life isn't perfect. Life is full of detours. Sometimes those detours are God-made detours. Sometimes those detours are man-made detours, and sometimes those detours are self-made detours. I have taken those self-made detours a time or two in my life, but I have discovered the juncture I find myself in at this point in time is the intersection of my self-made paths and the paths God has marked out for my life. Every event, every action, and every road taken has led me to this point. I also know God will not waste any road, or roadblock, or detour. Everything has made me into who I am today. Jesus has led me to mountaintops, He has been with me in the valleys, and He has walked me through the valley of the shadow of death. As I said before, "All roads lead somewhere." All those roads I have taken have led me here to this point of writing this book. Sometimes I don't get to see the whole map. Sometimes, I have to trust this path will lead me to God.

My verses for today: "Oh, that we might know the Lord! Let us press on to know him. He will respond to us as surely as the arrival of dawn or the coming of rains in early spring" Hosea 6:3 NLT.

"So let us acknowledge him! Let us seek to acknowledge the Lord! He will come to our rescue as certainly as the appearance of the dawn, as certainly as the winter rain comes, as certainly as the spring rain that waters the land" Hosea 6:3 NET.

If I want to know that I am on the right path God has for me, I need to ask myself this one question, "Am I doing all I can to press on to know Him more?" "Am I pursuing and chasing after God to know Him by experience in my mind, body, spirit, and heart?'

For Joseph, Mary, and Jesus, all paths led back to Nazareth.

Nazareth - the town Mary lived in before this whole adventure began. Nazareth – the place where the angel Gabriel came to Mary and explained to her the Lord's plan of salvation. Gabriel didn't tell Mary all the detours this path would take her on. He just explained the Holy Spirit would overshadow her. God would put His Son inside of her. That was it. She did not ask to see all this life would look like, she said, "Let it be done to me as God has said."

Joseph didn't ask to see all the places this path would lead him, but every time the angel said, "Get up and do ____," Joseph got up immediately and did what he was told to do. He knew whatever the Lord directed him to do was the path the Lord was going to use to protect the precious child in his care.

All the days ordained for Jesus were written in God's Book before one of them came to be. Hundreds of years before the birth of Jesus, God told the prophet Hosea that He would call His Son out of Egypt so God told Joseph to go to Egypt. "When Israel was a child, then I loved him and called My son out of Egypt." Hosea 11:1. In Egypt, Jesus was protected from Herod's massacre. Jesus was sent to the earth as God's Anointed. God sent Jesus to Nazareth. This would fulfill Messianic prophecy. Jesus' earthly life was all mapped out before one of them came to be. Sure, there were detours, but those detours were part of God's path.

All the days ordained for me were written in God's book before one of them came into existence. God has a map and a big picture for each of our lives. He sees beyond our vanishing point. We will experience detours and roadblocks, but God's got this. We have to search Him out. He will be faithful and He will be just. He will point us in the right direction.

The right path for our lives is the one that leads to knowing God more and more!

Questions to ponder and store in your heart:

Where did God tell Joseph to take Jesus?

Are you on God's path for your life?

As you reflect back over these past 40 days, what can you do to change directions and get on the road that leads to God?

What can you do to pursue God?

"Lord lead me on. Give me a passion to know You more and more, and to live in a vibrant relationship with the One who created me and saved me."

Dear Reader,

Thanks for reading along. I pray you have drawn closer to the True Reason for this Season. I hope these forty days have proofed your faith and you can say without a doubt that God still answers prayers, His time of waiting has a purpose, and Jesus still comes into the messiness and darkness of our lives.

Many missed that first Christmas. Herod held onto his kingship too tightly and missed worshipping the True King of Israel. Caesar Augustus was too infatuated with his power to ever worship another King. The people of Bethlehem were too busy to stop and worship.

My warning: Slow down, humble yourselves, and worship the True King of Kings and Lord of Lords.

Join me at www.unearthingtheeternityseed.com for discussions each day during these forty days of Christmas.

The profits from this book will go to a ministry that is very dear to me and my husband. We sit on the board of IAMNOT4GOTTEN Ministries. The insert is picture and a short bio of a child we help sponsor in Addis Ababa, Ethiopia. All I ask is that you would pray for the child in your copy of this book. Their lives are hard and devastating. They so desperately need a prayer warrior like you.

If you bought this book online and would like to become a prayer warrior, please message me at the above address and I will send you a child to pray for.

Kellye Jones

Enjoy this preview of

On
the
Way

**40 DAYS OF TRAVELING ON THE WAY
THROUGH THE COUNTRYSIDE WITH
JESUS DURING HIS EARLIEST DAYS
OF PUBLIC MINISTRY.**

Kellye Jones

They lived His adventure from their side of history. They woke up each morning with the probability of seeing water turned into wine, or witnessing the heavens open up and hearing a voice say, "This is my beloved Son." They lived a life worth living. They had no clue when they began the journey that they would see the blind receive sight, the deaf gain hearing, lepers become clean, and the dead raised to life. They followed Jesus of Nazareth from the courts of the temple, through the hills of Judea and the water wells of Samaria. They knew first hand the love and compassion of Jesus because they witnessed the love and compassion of Jesus on a daily basis.

Join me "On the way" and follow Jesus from their side of history. Don't pack any bags. You won't need them. All you need to follow Jesus on the way is an open seeking heart, and he will give you the adventure of a lifetime, and a story that is worth telling the world.

"Jesus told them, "Take nothing for the journey—no staff, no bag, no bread, no money, no extra shirt" Luke 9:3 NIV.